WHAT PEOPLE ARE SAYING ABOUT FRANKIE MAZZAPICA AND *YOUR DIVINE INVITATION*...

I first met Frankie Mazzapica over twenty years ago in Rockford, Illinois, when he was training youth pastors on how to be effective leaders with the renowned youth leader Jeanne Mayo. That's why it is no surprise to me that Frankie is now training people all around the world on the power of prayer through his insightful book, *Your Divine Invitation*. This book will help you become an effective prayer warrior, but it will also give you insight into becoming a better all-around leader.

Over the past ten years, I have been privileged to lead worship at Pastor Frankie's church on and off. At one service a few years ago, a guest went into full cardiac arrest and literally died on the platform during service while Frankie was interviewing her. I witnessed Frankie praying life over the lifeless woman, who was miraculously brought back to life. Pastor Frankie is a man who knows how to pray and believes what he teaches. I am honored to endorse this book for anyone who wants to grow in their relationship with Christ and walk with an understanding of God's supernatural power through prayer.

—*Ricardo Sanchez*
Worship leader; recording artist; Grammy Award nominee
Winner of Dove, Tejano Music, and ASCAP awards

Does God offer Christians supernatural power? If so, what is the purpose of this power, and how can one receive it? The church of today stands divided on these questions. Some would say that God no longer *empowers* believers as He once did. Others would say that He does but often fails to communicate how to receive it, and people misunderstand the purpose of the power. In his book *Your Divine Invitation*, Frankie answers these questions with biblical clarity. He also gives real-life examples of how an impartation of God's power completely changed his ministry, his church, and the lives of thousands who have been beneficiaries of God's power at work in Celebration Church. This book is a must for the person who truly wants to live out the divine call of being a *power-filled* witness of Jesus Christ.

—*Matt Scott*
Founding pastor, the Gathering Place Church
Birmingham, AL

Pastor Frankie has been an anointed guiding light in my family's spiritual journey for over a decade. His God-given message inspires hope, faith, and an overarching belief in God's plan for each of us. Frankie paints a bold vision that we must each seek and derive our power from God and the Holy Spirit. Only then will we truly be able to fulfill our divine assignment here on Earth. Through this book, Frankie guides us to desire the closeness of the Lord—not settling for anything less. My prayer is that this book will leave many blessed with a renewed conviction to achieve their full potential in their walk with the Lord and, most of all, learn to believe in miracles.

—*Dr. Lee M. Tillman*
Chairman, president, and CEO, Marathon Oil Corp.

This book illuminates the roadmap for every believer to engage in the supernatural in their everyday life. Pastor Frankie takes the reader along his journey from someone who rarely experienced healings to someone who witnesses them on a weekly basis. His story is an undeniable testimony of the power of God working today through anyone who asks, seeks, and knocks. This book will surely stir your hunger for more of the Holy Spirit to work through your life.

—*Micah Gamboa*
Executive director, Elijah Rising, Houston, TX

This book is a download from a man's secret place. We must be empowered by the Spirit. Why? We live in one of the most pivotal times in history for the believer. We must stand firm and walk in boldness. There is a constant attack from Satan on every front to bring the church and the bride of Christ down. As you read this book, your spirit will soar, and elements of your faith will be restored. *Your Divine Invitation* is a handbook to understand the Holy Spirit's weapons imparted into you for your victory. Now is the time to walk in the Spirit. Are you ready? Prepare to embark on the Luke 24:49 and Acts 1:8 journey into the enduement of power!

—*Pat Schatzline*
Author and evangelist
Remnant Ministries International, Fort Worth, TX

So many believers are unknowingly missing the *power* component of their *purpose* equation. Frankie brilliantly makes a case for the need for the power of the Holy Spirit from on high, but he also walks you through the *how* and the hard questions when it comes to actually receiving and activating that power in your life. Being in the business world and in ministry, this book was a timely reminder for me personally of how essential that power actually is to complete my mission on this earth. Thank you for your obedience and openness to the Spirit of God, Frankie!

—*Dan Valentine*
Healthy lifestyle specialist, entrepreneur
Motivational speaker, success mentor, global wellness coach

This book our friend has written completely lines up with who we know him to be. Three words come to mind: honest, courageous, and committed. Frankie is honest in his writing about what he has learned and has still yet to learn. He is courageous in taking steps of faith that many of us would be too timid to take in believing for God to do great things. He is committed to pursuing who God is and what He wants to accomplish through His children.

—*Greg and Janna Long*
Worship leaders; recording artists, Avalon Worship
Grammy nominees; American Music and Dove award winners

With *Your Divine Invitation*, Pastor Frankie takes readers on a wonderful journey of humility, transparency, and vulnerability to allow them to grow and develop in the power of Christ, regardless of their starting point. He continually seeks to understand and has an uncanny ability to connect as "one of us," seamlessly weaving Scriptures throughout. Frankie provides a credible foundation and a practical approach for readers to understand and act on this promise from God. These insights are wise beyond his years. I can't wait to read it again for that next revelation!

—*Adam Cantu*
Health/safety manager, global projects, ExxonMobil

Reneé and I have witnessed thousands of people receiving the baptism of the Holy Spirit and their lives being radically changed as a result. However, of the many who were privileged to have such an experience, only a few were truly *endued with power*. Too often, the emphasis was placed on speaking in tongues rather than receiving an impartation of power. Pastor Frankie Mazzapica has locked in on a vital key of ministry today; being empowered with the Spirit, as evidenced by signs and wonders, is needed now more than ever. *Your Divine Invitation* has rekindled a deep hunger for a fresh impartation of power in my life and our churches. People desperately need it, and the times demand it. Thank you, Pastor Frankie, for writing this masterpiece on the empowerment of the Holy Spirit today.

—*Randy and Reneé Clark*
Founding pastors, Triumph Church
Stafford, Nederland, and Beaumont, TX

Sometimes a book enters your life by divine intervention. I dare to believe that to be true for you as you read *Your Divine Invitation*. Some authors are just TV famous. But Frankie is that and far, far more for me. He is my son in the Lord, with whom I've been closely knit for over twenty years. The call of God on his life has been radiant since he was a young, rebellious kid who ran my sports car off the road in the middle of a snowstorm. He has always had the courage to say what he believes to be true, even if it is not entirely socially acceptable. Living up close to him, I have now had the priceless privilege to see him exercise all the Holy Spirit's gifts he speaks of in this book.

My background is five full decades in full-time ministry, so I am not easily impressed or manipulated. But in truth, Jesus uses Frankie in one of the purest, most authentic ways I have ever experienced in my entire life. He gently but authoritatively moves in the gifts of the Spirit. He is big enough to say when he is occasionally off, "I must have missed it." But more times than I can count, he is unmistakably *on*. The lasting fruit of his ministry shouts to prove it. Enjoy this book with a good cup of coffee and know that if you allow for it, it could irrevocably change your entire life. There is truly *more* to following Jesus and the fullness of the Spirit than many of us begin to realize.

—Dr. Jeanne Mayo
Public speaker, international author
President and founder, Youth Leader's Coach

YOUR

DIVINE

INVITATION

FRANKIE MAZZAPICA

YOUR
DIVINE
INVITATION

ACCESS THE HOLY SPIRIT
TO COMPLETE YOUR ASSIGNMENT

WHITAKER
HOUSE

YOUR DIVINE INVITATION
Access the Holy Spirit to Complete Your Assignment

Celebration Church of The Woodlands
6565 Research Forest Drive
The Woodlands, TX 77381
woodlandscelebration.com
frankiemazzapica.com

ISBN: 978-1-64123-916-5
eBook ISBN: 978-1-64123-917-2
Printed in the United States of America
© 2022 by Frankie Mazzapica

Whitaker House
1030 Hunt Valley Circle • New Kensington, PA 15068
www.whitakerhouse.com

LC record available at https://lccn.loc.gov/2022024359
LC ebook record available at https://lccn.loc.gov/2022024360

1 2 3 4 5 6 7 8 9 10 11 Ш**Ш** 29 28 27 26 25 24 23 22

DEDICATION

Allie, I thank God for the blind date He arranged in heaven for us. The moment I saw you, I wanted to marry you. You're my heartbeat. My love. My best friend. *You're the only one I need.*

Preslee, since the day you were born, we knew the anointing on your life was profoundly special. Our loving, honest, and transparent conversations will always be the golden moments of my life. *Who's the leader?*

Luke, you're my first mate. There is no one on Earth like you. You're perfect. I will forever guard every memory we've made together. *You're just like me except better.*

Kate, our family needed you to be complete. It seems all the gifts from heaven have been given to you. Everyone loves being around you, and that will be the experience of your life. *Your hugs bring me joy.*

Allie, Preslee, Luke, and Kate, I pray the words on these pages will be forever branded on your heart.

CONTENTS

FOREWORD

I first heard of Frankie several years ago when my secretary told me about a pastor from Celebration Church in The Woodlands, Texas, who had requested one hour of my time and would fly anywhere in the world to meet me and get needed answers. Frankie's hunger reminded me of my own at thirty-two years old. I once sent a letter to John Wimber stating that I wanted to be one of his interns. I wrote that I was willing to sell my home and buy a camper, park it on the church lot, and serve for a year without any salary if John would approve. I detected in Frankie's offer a similar hunger. John had not needed another intern, so my offer was rejected. I did not reject Frankie's offer though. I agreed to meet with him.

He came with a list of questions, especially about being filled or baptized with the Holy Spirit and if receiving an impartation was like being filled or baptized in the Spirit. We spent the hour talking. When his alarm went off, he ended his questions and started to leave. I told him I would give him another hour. We talked about the ways of God, and I gave him many of my books. I also told him that he should join me in Brazil if he wanted to have a breakthrough in healing.

Frankie did join me and brought a couple other people from his staff. That trip to Belo Horizonte was transformative. I had him sit by me a lot on the trip. He was like a child in a candy store—so excited and amazed at what God was doing. We always counted the number of healings that happened through the team on one of the three buses. Frankie counted one side and I counted the other. I will never forget when he cried out to me with wide eyes, "Dr. Randy, there are more healings on my side of the bus than I have seen in my entire life, and this is only half of the bus, and there are three buses." He invited over one hundred of Celebration Church's prayer partners the following year. Thirty-eight were able to come with us. That next year, in Fortaleza, Brazil, their team alone nearly filled one of our four chartered buses.

The next major milestone in our journey together was when Frankie invited me to come to teach in his church for a weekend. Due to airline problems, I was not going to make it in time for the service's start. I called Frankie and told him this had happened at another church in Texas and that he should study the training manual and lead the service that he had advertised. I would get there when I could, hopefully not more than a couple of hours late. I told Frankie that God would back him up—just step out and go for it.

Frankie declined my advice. Instead, his church staff sent a mass text and email and blitzed social media, informing everyone that service would start an hour late. I arrived after the worship was over; they had extended it beyond the regular length to give me time to get there. What a night that was. Frankie accused me of teaching the information from three healing schools in one service. I really didn't do that, but I did want to help break Frankie through into the more of God.

I came off the platform to where Frankie and his wife Allie were seated in the front row as I was speaking. I whispered in their ears, "In a few minutes, I am going to invite you two onto the platform. I want each of you to give five words of knowledge for healing." They were shocked, but they knew I would do what I said. When I called them up, they stepped out in faith and gave the words. During this time, I sat in the front row and coached them on what to do when people responded to the words of knowledge and coached them in the prayer ministry for healing. As a result, God was faithful, and people were healed.

Then I asked Frankie if he had trained any of his ministry team. He told me that he had, but they had never had an opportunity to give words in a worship service. So I invited the members of Frankie's ministry team to come forward, saying that God would give them words of knowledge and people would be healed when they prayed. Again, God was faithful, and people were healed through Frankie's ministry team.

Frankie had seen about thirty or forty healings in his church since Brazil. That weekend we saw over two hundred healings in three services. Since that weekend, they have seen healings take place in every service, not just in special healing meetings. Just as Frankie was, the thirty-eight prayer partners had been powerfully impacted in Brazil. When they came home, they brought their faith to the local church.

Three people attended Frankie and Allie's first service when they launched their church in a small community center thirteen years earlier. Now, Frankie begins to do what I did with my church. I would take members out with me to be part of the ministry team at other churches, where I would do training on healing and the gifts of the Spirit. Frankie discovered God's faithfulness to meet those who would step out in faith. He also learned how giving opportunities to the members of his church to heal would contribute to their growth in faith and how to co-labor with God.

Frankie not only has a transformed life, he has a transformed church. Celebration Church was already a fast-growing church with three Sunday morning services. Now though, ministry is so much more exciting for Frankie and the members of his church. For them, *"Christ in you, the hope of glory"* (Colossians 1:27 NIV) rings true.

Like the apostle Paul, Frankie is learning about *"the mystery that has been kept hidden for ages and generations, but is now disclosed to the Lord's people. To them God has chosen to make known among the Gentiles the glorious riches of this mystery, which is Christ in you, the hope of glory. He is the one we proclaim, admonishing and teaching everyone with all wisdom, so that we may present everyone fully mature in Christ. To this end I strenuously contend with all the energy Christ so powerfully works in me"* (Colossians 1:26–29 NIV).

Healings are signs of the inbreaking of the kingdom that accompany the preaching of Jesus. Him we proclaim! To us, the mystery of the kingdom has been revealed; it is Christ in us, *"the hope of glory."* Oh, to be a co-laborer with Jesus—how wonderful to know that you *"will lay hands on the sick, and they will recover"* (Mark 16:18 NKJV), to know that Jesus has prayed for us.

One thing I need to mention: Frankie wanted to have a powerful experience like Charles Finney had when Finney was baptized in the Holy Spirit. As far as I know, Frankie has not had a powerful experience of being knocked down and electrocuted. But he *has* been anointed. God has been training him, building his understanding of working with the Holy Spirit. God is powerfully using Frankie. I look forward to his weekly Sunday morning reports on what happened in his church. I'm not sure when he started, but Frankie now calls me, leaving video messages almost every Sunday. He tells me what he thinks God will do or tells me about the healings and miracles that he saw in his church that day. Sometimes, he asks more questions. In my fifty-one years of ministry, as of November 2021, I have only met a handful of pastors with such hunger for more of God, hunger to see His power bring Him glory. Frankie stands out among this handful of leaders.

What can you learn from Frankie, especially if you are a pastor or leader?

1. Follow the urgings of the Holy Spirit.

2. Be humble enough to realize when you don't understand something or how to move in certain gifts of the Spirit.

3. Reach out to someone who can become a coach to you.

4. Take members of your staff when you expect to have the possibility of a powerful experience in/with God.

5. Take your ministry team someplace where they will be exposed to lots of power to heal and for impartation, where they can become part of the ministry team to experience God using them, not mere spectators.

6. Bring ministers who can teach, train, activate gifts, and impart to your church to expose your congregation, especially your ministry team, to a healing ministry.

7. Find someone you trust, who believes in you and will be willing to be a sounding board and coach as you continue to grow in operating in the gifts and the ministry of healing.

8. Don't be satisfied with a breakthrough. Be thankful but keep asking for more.

9. Stay humble. God will resist the proud.

10. Be authentic. If you're unsure, don't pretend you are sure. Be honest.

11. Make it a goal for your life, ministry, and church to equip others in what you are learning. You don't want to become God's man of power for the hour. You want to become the pastor of a great church of power for the hour. Equip the saints for the work of ministry.

Your Divine Invitation is an amazing call to enter and experience the realm of the supernatural. Read this book and learn from a great student who is becoming a great teacher-mentor. You will not be disappointed, and you will enjoy the journey with Frankie as your guide.

—*Dr. Randy Clark*
Founder, Global Awakening

ACKNOWLEDGMENTS

Dad, if it were not for my dear relationship with you, I would not be on the road I am.

Mom, thank you for the support, the encouragement, and mostly your endearing love.

Celebration Church, thank you for the privilege of being your pastor. It's been an exhilarating ride of learning, growing, and taking *risks* together. The Lord truly has made us a source of strength.

Sarah Stephens, thank you for being at the helm of the ministry the Lord has entrusted to us. Thanks to your efforts, this book will reach countless lives.

Dr. Randy, your mentorship has changed the trajectory of my life and ministry.

Christine Whitaker, thank you for believing in me as well as the message within this book. I'm humbled to be a part of the Whitaker family.

Suvwe Kokoricha, thank you for editing the manuscript for this book. You are the one who carried this work across the finish line.

INTRODUCTION

My search for more of God began with insomnia. One night in 2018, I lay wide awake in bed, waiting for sleep to come, but it did not. A little past midnight, I pulled out my phone and started looking for something to read. I remember scrolling through, looking for a book engaging enough that it would not be a waste of my money but so boring that it would put me to sleep. It did not take long before I found *Power from God* by

Charles Finney.[1] When I saw the book, I thought, "There's a 100 percent chance that this guy's going to put me to sleep." And for that, I was grateful.

I bought the book and began reading. I had not planned on reading more than a few chapters that night—just enough to lull me to sleep. But I kept reading after those first few chapters. I kept reading until I had nearly finished the book. It was four in the morning when I reached its end. Finney's book had marked me. In his book, he wrote about Luke 24:49 (KJV): *"Behold, I send the promise of my Father upon you: but tarry ye in the city of Jerusalem, until ye be endued with power from on high."* I had read that verse before, but reading it again left me with a niggling feeling that I had not even scratched the surface of its meaning.

I do not remember a time when the church was not a significant part of my life. I grew up in my parents' Pentecostal church in Negaunee, Michigan. When I was seven, my parents resigned as senior pastors and became evangelists. We spent the next five years traveling. When I was twelve, my parents became associate pastors at a church in Houston. I stayed there with them until I was eighteen. I graduated high school and then went to Rockford, Illinois, for a gap year that turned into a three-year ministerial internship. I took Bible college courses while there, and I have been pastoring ever since. I began in youth ministry, where I served for eight years until 2005, when my wife Allie and I planted Celebration Church in The Woodlands, Texas. Yet, for years, I knew nothing about an impartation of power.

---

1. Charles Finney, *Power from God* (New Kensington, PA: Whitaker House, 1996).

All I could say to people facing addiction, disease, or a broken marriage was, "I'll be praying for you." I felt helpless. I wanted to do more—to see more. I wanted to see God move upon them when I prayed. I wanted to see miracles happen in their lives.

This book is for the believer with that same desire—the believer who wants to be a conduit for God's love and power, letting those things flow out of them into others in a moment. This book is for those who say, "If the power of God is available—I want it!" I wrote the following chapters for those frustrated with the single dimension of God they are currently experiencing.

The belief that only a small few are selected to receive God's supernatural power is a fallacy. God knows that before we have anything to offer, we must have His power. Jesus told the disciples not to start their ministry until they had been *"endued with power from on high"* (Luke 24:49 KJV). We have the same assignment the disciples did. If they needed power then, we need power now. I am not inviting you to be weird or incomprehensible. Jesus was neither of those things, so we should not be those things either. Jesus healed countless individuals, delivered people from evil spirits, and performed miracles. If you read chapters two, three, and four in the Gospel of Mark, you will notice that thousands of people followed Jesus wherever He went. Jesus was not weird. He was magnetic. To do as He did, we must be approachable like He was.

Each of us has the responsibility to share what we have with the rest of the world. If we are not careful, our persona and *Christianese* will cause us to become enigmatic. None of us can

THE BELIEF THAT ONLY A
SMALL FEW ARE SELECTED TO
RECEIVE GOD'S SUPERNATURAL
POWER IS A FALLACY. GOD
KNOWS THAT BEFORE WE HAVE
ANYTHING TO OFFER, WE MUST
HAVE HIS POWER.

afford to become so weird that we lose any hope of having divine influence. Jesus said:

> *You are the salt of the earth. But what good is salt if it has lost its flavor? Can you make it salty again? It will be thrown out and trampled underfoot as worthless.*
>
> (Matthew 5:13)

"Worthless" is a strong word. I have seen people try to stand up for God by getting into shouting matches. I have seen people be so dogmatic that they become repelling. Each time, I think, *I do not believe Jesus would have done this that way if He were here.* Scripture tells us that Jesus never fought, shouted, or raised His voice in public. (See Matthew 12:19.)

If we live our lives like Jesus, we will be both powerful and approachable. People invited their friends and walked for hours from surrounding regions to hear what He had to say. (See Mark 3:7–8.) Even *"disreputable sinners"* (Mark 2:15) wanted to be around Jesus. As bold and plain-spoken as he was, John the Baptist still had a following of unbelievers who would happily listen to him, including King Herod. (See Mark 6:20.)

So often, we go to such great lengths to avoid offending nonbelievers. We dress like them, talk like them, and do whatever else we can to be relatable, thinking that is the secret to drawing them toward the Lord. This could not be further from the truth. The message of Jesus Christ should be straightforward; more importantly, it should be given in love. Hear my heart—the message and the messenger are not mysterious or weird. Scripture is clear that we will exhibit a contrast to the people we are trying to reach with the gospel. *"For what do righteousness and wickedness have in common?"* (2 Corinthians 6:14 NIV).

It can be challenging to find a church that strikes this balance—that is both growing steadily and operating in the gifts. It has been my experience that if a church moves in the gifts of the Spirit, they are not growing. For example, I grew up in a traditional Pentecostal church. Every Sunday, the gift of tongues could be heard throughout the service, with a congregation of about a hundred people. The only time we grew was when someone had a baby.

However, if we look closely at Jesus's ministry, He operated in all of the gifts, and He had no problems reaching the lost and building up believers. Jesus spent three years on the earth doing ministry to show us how to reach our friends and loved ones. He said, *"I have set you an example that you should do as I have done for you"* (John 13:15 NIV). Jesus moved in the gifts, and His ministry multiplied faster than any modern-day church. When the gifts are real, undeniable, and demonstrated the way Jesus modeled them—simply, with love and without hype—people will line up for miles.

I believe that we will never be at peace and genuinely fulfilled until we are doing what we are born to do: share the love and power of God with as many people as possible. I once believed that goal could be accomplished merely by living a holy and attractive life and encouraging others to have "quiet time" with the Lord each day. Such things are of paramount

WE WILL NEVER BE AT PEACE AND GENUINELY FULFILLED UNTIL WE ARE DOING WHAT WE ARE BORN TO DO: SHARE THE LOVE AND POWER OF GOD WITH AS MANY PEOPLE AS POSSIBLE.

importance, though without the manifest power of God, we will always be working harder than we should, with less fruit than we ought to have. God is always ready to give us more of Himself so that we may be a part of the remnant who will feel the Word of the Lord burning in our hearts as Jeremiah did. (See Jeremiah 20:9.) Such fire can and should flow from us and instantly spark a manifestation of God's power when we pray in the name of Jesus. It is past time for believers everywhere to impact those around them with power and the demonstration of the Holy Spirit.

Jesus said, *"I tell you the truth, anyone who believes in me will do the same works I have done, and even greater works, because I am going to be with the Father"* (John 14:12). Let us not explain away or overlook these Scriptures anymore. We are called to more. In the first thirty-nine years of my life, I can only think of one instant, miraculous healing that happened the moment I prayed. Now, a miracle does not happen every time I pray, but every week, people are miraculously healed the moment I call on Jesus. If an impartation of power can happen to me, it can happen to you.

Throughout this book, I will use the words *impartation* and *endowment* interchangeably. Both are defined as the giving and receiving of spiritual gifts, blessings, healing, and baptism in the Holy Spirit to build up the church's work of the ministry. The basis for impartation and spiritual endowments is well-established doctrine and stated plainly by Paul to the early church in Rome:

For I long to see you, that I may impart to you some spiritual gift to strengthen you. (Romans 1:11 ESV)

That is where my journey began, and I think that is the best place to start you on yours.

SECTION I

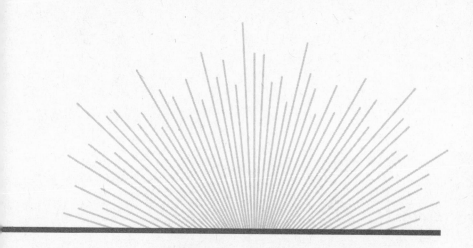

POWER TO COMPLETE YOUR ASSIGNMENT

1

AN IMPARTATION CHANGES EVERYTHING

Why do so many prayers go unanswered? That question used to plague me—and it did not stop plaguing me when I was a youth pastor or even when I planted Celebration Church with Allie. Our church checked all of the boxes: great worship, exciting kids' services, and sermons that connected with people. But that question still lingered. I did not see healings and miracles like the ones mentioned in Scripture happening in my church.

Spiritual gifts strengthened neither my ministry nor my personal life. And I wanted to know why.

I asked every pastor I knew why I was not seeing a manifestation of God's power. No one had an answer for me, but that did not stop my search. Scripture gives many instances of believers everywhere experiencing the supernatural when they prayed, not just the apostles. For example, *"Stephen, a man full of God's grace and power, performed amazing miracles and signs"* (Acts 6:8). He moved in power as he went about distributing food to widows. (See Acts 6:1–6.)

Other supporting Scriptures include:

Everything is possible for one who believes.

(Mark 9:23 NIV)

I tell you the truth, anyone who believes in me will do the same works I have done, and even greater works, because I am going to be with the Father. (John 14:12)

Such a prayer offered in faith will heal the sick, and the Lord will make you well. And if you have committed any sins, you will be forgiven. (James 5:15)

Everyone who reads the Bible must decide what they will do with the portions that they do not understand. Will they pursue a revelation of truth? Or will they turn a blind eye and learn to live without the manifestation of God's power? I made my choice after finishing Finney's book.

MIDNIGHT REVELATION

After midnight, when I had put down *Power from God*, I was lying in bed, unable to fall asleep. So, I opened the Bible app on my phone and began reading. As I read, I noticed something I had never seen before: the word "power" is laced throughout the New Testament. As I jumped from book to book, chapter to chapter, I realized that many new believers had faith yet no power. When they did receive power, though, everything changed.

After John baptized Jesus, *"God anointed Jesus of Nazareth with the Holy Spirit and with power"* (Acts 10:38). Jesus showed that power when He changed water into wine at the wedding feast in Cana of Galilee. (See John 2:1–11.) Seeing that miracle may have given the disciples more faith, but they still lacked power.

> *One day Jesus called together his twelve disciples and gave them power and authority to cast out all demons and to heal all diseases.* (Luke 9:1)

Later, Jesus selected seventy-two other followers who already possessed faith and gave them the power to heal (see Luke 10:1–9) so that they could fulfill the Great Commission. (See Matthew 28:19–20.)

Jesus gave His followers an impartation of power to lessen the weight brought on by the Great Commission. He told them that they would *"receive power"* when the Holy Spirit came upon them, becoming His witnesses and telling people about Him *"everywhere—in Jerusalem, throughout Judea, in Samaria, and to the ends of the earth"* (Acts 1:8).

In Acts 4:29, just after the disciples prayed for *"great boldness in preaching,"* power again came upon them, and the ground began to shake. (See verse 31.) The manifestation of that power is outlined ten chapters later. After preaching in Iconium, *"the Lord proved their message was true by giving them power to do miraculous signs and wonders"* (Acts 14:3).

It was no different with Paul's ministry. When he and those with him preached the gospel, it was *"not only in word, but also in power and in the Holy Spirit and with full conviction"* (1 Thessalonians 1:5 ESV).

Yet, in their eagerness to jump into ministry, many still choose to preach, teach, and witness without waiting for an impartation of power. Paul wrote a message for such people:

> *I will come—and soon—if the Lord lets me, and then I'll find out whether these arrogant people just give pretentious speeches or whether they really have God's power. For the Kingdom of God is not just a lot of talk; it is living by God's power.* (1 Corinthians 4:19–20)

While reading the Bible on my cell phone with Allie sleeping next to me, I concluded that miracles could happen

IN JESUS'S NAME, SOME MAY PROPHESY, CAST OUT DEMONS, AND PERFORM MIRACLES. YET WITHOUT RELATIONSHIP, JESUS WILL SAY TO THEM, "GET AWAY FROM ME."

through a person who has not received an impartation of power. However, an impartation is needed if such signs are to be a regular occurrence.

Aside from an impartation of power, we must have a relationship with Jesus. In His name, some may prophesy, cast out demons, and perform miracles. (See Matthew 7:22.) Yet without relationship, Jesus will say to them, *"Get away from me, you who break God's laws"* (Matthew 7:23). We all need our faith to increase, and each of us must have His power flowing through us. As we unpack the Word together, you will see that an impartation of power is available to all believers.

AN IMPARTATION OF POWER

An impartation of power made all the difference in Celebration Church and my life. I first saw miracles happen through my prayers on a mission trip to Brazil with Dr. Randy Clark. The big decision for me after that trip was choosing to believe that the power of God could travel over the ocean and heal the people I prayed for when I preached. The Sunday I got back, I felt God saying to me, "Go for a word of knowledge." That scared me. It was a risk to put myself on the line. I drew out my sermon as much as I could to delay ministry time. But I could only draw it out so much.

When the time came, I led with, "I do not know if this is God, or if it is me. I do know that if it is God, someone is about to get healed." Then, I gave two words of knowledge. Both people were healed when they were prayed for at the front. The following Sunday, I had them come up and share their testimonies. Then, I gave more words of knowledge and saw those people get healed. As a church, we have been following that same pattern ever since.

Before that, miraculous healings were rare in my life. Now, I expect them. Not everyone I pray for receives healing, but people are healed every Sunday. I may never understand why some people receive their miracle the first time we pray for them while others receive theirs the fiftieth time. Or why some people never receive their healing despite never losing faith for their miracle. Honestly, I have more questions than answers.

However, one thing is certain: we *have* received a breakthrough. It does not matter whether a staff pastor or one of our many prayer partners prays over the sick. We see the manifest power of God every Sunday. Most weekends, I lose count of how many people received their healing. Miracles are not just for Sunday services though. God wants to move through you wherever you are, whether miracles are your focus at that time or not.

One of my favorite healing stories began without healing expectations on my part.

A CIRCLE OF HEALING

In June 2020, Allie and I visited our friends Luke and Serena in their second home in Costa Rica. Because they do a lot of business in Costa Rica, they bought the home more than twenty years ago. Both in Texas and abroad, this amazing couple lives out their call to full-time ministry without even receiving a salary from Celebration Church. I can count on one hand the number of times Luke has been absent from my biweekly men's life group, and Serena is a cornerstone of our prayer partner time. Together, they lead a weekly life group in their home. They are fully committed to building God's kingdom, and they still find time to lead a very successful company that they built themselves. Like the apostle Paul and his tent-making business, their occupation is a tool to provide for their family and invest in the kingdom. They invited Allie and me to Costa Rica to minister to their *tico* friends. (*Tico* is an affectionate term used for dear friends and loved ones who live in Costa Rica.)

In addition to our two families, three couples sat with us on a covered patio. Everyone there seemed to be between the ages of forty-five and fifty-five. Each *tico* stole my heart immediately. We talked and laughed a lot. As we traded pleasantries, it became clear that although they were all Christians, they were young in the faith. After a bit more small talk, I began to share a few Scriptures I believed would bless them. About fifteen or twenty minutes later, I had said all I had to say, and I was ready to close up the evening. However, the night felt undone.

A quick thought crossed my mind, "Go for healing." Revelation 19:10 (ESV) says, "*The testimony of Jesus is the spirit of prophecy*," so I started sharing recent testimonies of how people had been healed at our church over the last few years. I told them how Jesus was healing people at our church every weekend. I explained that though not everyone we prayed for received healing, people did get healed each Sunday. Sometimes they were healed the first time we prayed for them and sometimes we had to pray for them many more times, but most often, they were healed the very moment they came to the altar. I told them that I believed healings were going to happen that night. Then I asked, "Is there anyone here who needs healing?"

To my surprise, three of our six guests raised their hands. "Okay, we're going to pray for each of you," I said. "Is there anyone feeling pain right now? We want to pray for you first." Diana was the first to raise her hand. She said she had been experiencing sharp pain in her right hip, and it was shooting down her leg. We all stood up, and I asked her to come and stand in front of me. I said, "You're the first person I believe Jesus is going to heal tonight, and Serena will be the one to pray for you."

Asking Serena, our host, to come and pray was not a deliberate choice. I had intended to pray for Diana myself, but in that moment, it just seemed right that Serena would be the one to pray.

Just before Serena laid hands on Diana, I said to everyone, "Listen carefully to how Serena prays." I explained that her prayer would be a short, commanding prayer rather than a petition prayer. Then I explained the difference: petition prayers are based on requests to Jesus, while commanding prayers are based on speaking to the body and commanding it to be healed in Jesus's name.

Jesus most often healed the sick with commanding prayers. When He healed the lame man beside the pool of Bethesda, He said, "*Stand up, pick up your mat, and walk!*" (John 5:8). When He raised the widow's son from the dead, "*he walked over to the coffin and touched it, and the bearers stopped. 'Young man,' he said,*

'I tell you, get up'" (Luke 7:14). When He healed a man with leprosy, He said, *"Be healed!"* (Mark 1:41). Those were not long, effortful prayers. They were simple phrases said with God's power.

Serena had been through our prayer partner training and also prayed for the sick as part of our recent Brazil mission trip team, so I knew she would provide a great example of how to pray for the suffering the way Jesus did. After Serena prayed a thirty-second commanding prayer with great emphasis on saying, "in the name of Jesus," I asked Diana if she could feel any pain. She was surprised and in total disbelief when she realized her pain was gone. She did not understand how her healing could have happened that easily. We asked her to sit down, stand up, and move around to see if she was genuinely healed. Her eyes began to fill with tears. It did not matter how she shifted her body. There was no pain to be found! She was completely healed. We all took a moment to clap and praise Jesus. It was clear the Spirit of the Lord was among us, and faith was rapidly rising.

Patricia was next. I turned to Diana and said, "Diana, because you just received healing, you now have faith that Jesus heals. Listen to Patricia carefully because you are going to pray for her." Patricia then told us that her lower back was hurting and that her sinuses had been so bad for so long that she was unable to breathe through her nose. When Patricia finished telling us where she needed healing, Diana was noticeably nervous, but she was willing to do as I had asked. I reminded Diana to say a short prayer, commanding the parts of the body that

JESUS MOST OFTEN HEALED THE SICK WITH COMMANDING PRAYERS— SIMPLE PHRASES SAID WITH GOD'S POWER.

needed healing in the name of Jesus. As I spoke, I had a thought that made me wonder if Jesus had already healed Patricia's back.

"Patricia," I said, "sometimes Jesus heals before we have an opportunity to pray. I know you said you were feeling pain in your lower back a moment ago, but are you still feeling pain right now?" She took a moment to concentrate on her body and move her back around, and then said, "No, the pain is gone. What happened?" I smiled and laughed a bit, then answered, "Jesus, very often, doesn't wait on us. He just moves! Come on, everyone, let's give Him a standing ovation."

After clapping, I turned back to Diana. "Okay, Diana," I said. "Jesus went ahead of us on the healing of Patricia's back, but you still have an opportunity to partner with Him. Place your thumbs on each side of Patricia's nose and command it to open and command her sinuses to be completely healed in Jesus's name." Diana laid her hands on Patricia's face and prayed a quiet, commanding prayer over her. She ended her prayer with "in Jesus's name." Patricia closed her mouth and tried to breathe through her nose. Suddenly, she burst into tears and said, "Clear air is going all the way through my nose! It's so clear!" Crying, she walked over to her husband and threw her arms around him. Her life had changed instantly. We all gave Jesus another standing ovation.

So far, two people had been healed, and I, the pastor, had done none of the praying. First, Serena from our church prayed over Diana. Then, Diana prayed for Patricia. Now that Patricia had received her healing, it was her turn to pray for the next person: Catalina. I asked Catalina if she felt any pain. She said that she had the opposite problem. At some point in her life, she had lost all feeling in the skin of her thighs. There was also something seriously wrong with her stomach. Each time she ate, she vomited. On that particular day, she had decided not to eat to be sure she could accept the invitation to our gathering. I am always amazed by how easy it is for sharp, successful people to hide debilitating pains and diseases so well. The three couples I had just met all wore nice clothes and seemed to come from high-income families. All six were bilingual. Yet, those things did not matter in the presence of God.

I turned to Catalina and said, "Unlike the others, your sickness is internal, and it isn't causing you any pain. There is no way you can test whether you are healed by simply moving in ways you could not before praying. So, there are two ways you will know whether or not you are healed. First, after you leave tonight, you'll discover that you have feeling on the skin of your thighs, and after a meal, you will realize that you can digest your food without vomiting. Second, because you know your body, if Jesus touches the inside of you right now, you will instantly know it."

Looking at Patricia, I said, "When you pray, I want you to say, 'Skin, come alive. Nerves come alive. Stomach be healed, in the name of Jesus.'" As I said those words, Catalina grabbed her stomach, bent over, and began to moan as if her stomach was contracting. Then she started falling backward. Thankfully, there was a couch behind her that caught her fall. Her husband held her close, looking worried. I ignored the chaos because I was confident that God was doing something special beyond our understanding within her. We just needed to be patient and allow the process to unfold.

I still wanted the train of prayer to continue, though, so I asked Patricia to stand behind the couch Catalina was on, place one of her hands upon Catalina's shoulders, and pray. Catalina began to hyperventilate. Her eyes would close for several seconds at a time, and she would say, "I cannot move my arms." I got on my knees and held her hands tightly. As she squeezed my hands in response, I said, "Catalina, look into my eyes. Look at me. It's okay. Everything is okay. Jesus is healing you. Let's breathe slowly together; follow me. In and out. Very slow. That's it. Very good." Each time she looked away, her eyes would close, and she would hyperventilate again. And each time she hyperventilated, I said the same thing as before: "Catalina, look into my eyes and breathe with me."

The other couples started to get concerned. Someone asked, "Should we call someone?" I heard another person say, "Maybe she needs some water." I focused on Catalina the entire time, not responding to what I heard in the background. After three to five minutes of this, the biggest smile appeared on Catalina's face, and she started to laugh. "I'm healed!" she exclaimed. "I'm completely healed. I could eat a pig right now!"

We all started laughing too. Everything happened so quickly. We were all amazed. We could not even begin to process what had just happened. Catalina was full of joy—so full of joy that she stopped speaking in English and started speaking in Spanish. One of the others tried to interpret her words, but Catalina was talking too fast for interpretation. Her excitement made her words race out of her mouth. Having given up on understanding, we decided to stop trying and gave Jesus another standing ovation of praise as we raised our voices, saying, "Thank You, Jesus! Thank You, Jesus!"

When Catalina's emotions began to settle, I asked her to walk me through what had just happened to her. She said, "When you turned your head to tell Patricia to lay her hands on my stomach and say, 'Skin come alive, nerves come alive, stomach be healed,' there was a pain in my stomach, and in my mind, I saw an image of a hand with a knife chopping my stomach like someone chopping on a board. It was so painful! I thought, 'Someone is doing this to me.' Then I felt another hand grabbing me by the throat so that I couldn't breathe. Then I saw your hand and forearm, wrapped by the brightest white light. Brighter than that light." She pointed to the ceiling light above her. "Your hand reached into my stomach, and I heard an order. It was a firm order: 'Leave in Jesus's name!' Instantly, the hand around my neck let go, and the hand with the knife left my body."

Javier, Patricia's husband, spoke up then. "I didn't say anything earlier, but my knee has been giving me problems and causing me a lot of pain." I asked if he was feeling pain at that moment. He said yes. "Okay, Catalina," I said. "It's your turn. You were the last one to receive healing, and now it's your turn to pray for healing. Hold Javier's hands and pray a commanding prayer toward his knees. Name everything you think could be wrong—cartilage, muscles, tendons, bones. Command everything to be made well in the name of Jesus."

Catalina took Javier by the hand and started praying so simply that some might hesitate to call it a prayer. However, the

punctuation after the commanding prayer was greatly empha-
sized as she said, "In Jesus's name!" Javier started sitting and
standing to test his knee. He started laughing and said, "The
pain is gone!"

Other than Javier, everyone who had received healing that
night prayed for someone else who received their healing. I
believe that if there had been a hundred people in that room,
the prayer chain would have continued, and all of them would
have received healing. Ministry is so much more fun when you
partner with Jesus. Having a front-row seat to watch the power
of God move is the most incredible honor one could have.

God sent us each an invitation to partner with Him.

*He will keep you strong to the end so that you will be free
from all blame on the day when our Lord Jesus Christ
returns. God will do this, for he is faithful to do what he
says, and he has invited you into partnership with his Son,
Jesus Christ, our Lord.*   (1 Corinthians 1:8–9)

I promise, if you knew what this partnership could look like,
nothing else in this world would matter to you. When you experience the power of God instantly healing people or changing
their hearts and spirits through your prayers, you will become
addicted to the partnership. All you will want to do is spend
time with Him privately and share His love and power in public.

Although I do not fully understand how an impartation of
power happens, there is no doubt that a degree of power has
come upon our prayer partners, our congregation, and myself.

HAVING A FRONT-ROW SEAT TO
WATCH THE POWER OF GOD
MOVE IS THE MOST INCREDIBLE
HONOR ONE COULD HAVE.

The degree of impartation we have received has been significant enough to spark thousands of healings, ranging from the opening of deaf ears to deliverance from seizures. This degree of increased power has only caused greater hunger for more of God's manifest presence among us.

There is an unspeakable joy attached to seeing members in our congregation praying for one another and seeing the power of God move through and among them. It is a reminder to us all that God's plan is to send His power through and among all His children, not just through pastors, teachers, evangelists, prophets, and apostles. Prayerfully, within the pages of this book, you will come to understand all I have learned. In turn, you will see the power of God move through you too.

CHAPTER 1: DISCOVERY QUESTIONS

1. Why do you think it's rare to see healings and miracles?

_____

_____

_____

_____

_____

_____

2. What are your thoughts about the Scripture that reads: *"These miraculous signs will accompany those who believe: They will cast out demons in my name, and they will speak in new languages. They will be able to handle snakes with safety, and if they drink anything poisonous, it won't hurt them. They will be able to place their hands on the sick, and they will be healed"* (Mark 16:17–18).

_____

_____

_____

_____

_____

3. If those who were not in a relationship with Jesus could prophesy, cast out demons, and perform miracles using the name of Jesus (see Matthew 7:22), shouldn't those who are in relationship with Him expect, at the very least, to do the same?

_____

_____

_____

_____

_____

4. Jesus used commanding prayers when He healed the sick and cast out demons. (See, for example, John 5:8; John 9:6–7; Mark 1:25.) When would you deem it to be appropriate to use a commanding prayer? When would it be best to use a petitionary prayer?

_____

_____

_____

_____

_____

2

FAITH NEEDS POWER

The Bible says, *"You will receive power when the Holy Spirit comes upon you"* (Acts 1:8).

What exactly would the power of the Holy Spirit look like upon a person? It will flesh out differently in every believer, depending on their personality, character, and God-given assignment. Many people figure out how to live and do ministry without a manifestation of the Holy Spirit's power because they are unsure of what this power would look like in their lives. They lack clarity not only about the Holy Spirit's power, but also how it would appear in them. Thus, most figure out how to live and do ministry without a manifestation of power.

There is nothing to fear, however. When the Spirit of the Lord moves through people, they can make an impact beyond their natural abilities.

When the power of the Holy Spirit moves through you, human effort is minimal. The Holy Spirit's power changes everything. Charles Finney noted the great diversity of manifestations the Spirit of the Lord has in a person's life. I have included a few biblical examples, as well as some from myself and others. In addition to Finney's book *Power from God*, Pastor David Yonggi Cho's book *The Fourth Dimension*[2] and Dr. Randy Clark's book *There Is More*[3] are also great resources.

GOD SPEAKING TO AND THROUGH YOU

I remember lying in bed one day when I was about sixteen years old, going through my usual quiet time routine. I would pray for a few moments and then concentrate on opening my mind to receive thoughts from God. When God spoke to me this way, it always seemed as if I knew when my thoughts would stop and His thoughts would begin because I would have the thought, *I love you.* And then it was off to the races! Ideas would

2. Dr. David Yonggi Cho, *The Fourth Dimension* (Alachua, FL: Bridge-Logos Publishers, 2016).
3. Randy Clark, *There Is More!: The Secret to Experiencing God's Power to Change Your Life* (Bloomington, MN: Chosen Books, 2013).

WHEN THE SPIRIT OF THE LORD
MOVES THROUGH PEOPLE,
THEY CAN MAKE AN IMPACT
BEYOND THEIR
NATURAL ABILITIES.

come like a steady stream from the Lord just as long as my mind was on Him.

Until one day, I thought, *Come on, Frankie, that's not God. That's you talking to you. You're just making all this up in your mind.* Then it all came to an end. I would say my prayers and just roll over and go to sleep. This continued for a while until a lady I recognized but had never spoken with walked up to me while I was just leaning against a wall, hanging out with my friends. She told me, "Frankie, that voice you're hearing is God. Keep listening."

My mind was blown. How did she know? This lady was not the pastor's wife or a staff member. She looked like all the other middle-aged, single women who sat on the other side of the church. I will never forget that moment, not just because I was at such a formidable age, but because the way she heard from God at that moment has impacted my life to this day.

Our ability to hear from God and have His power flow through us is a game-changer. We must learn to live with this promised power. Not understanding the implications should not deter us. Perplexity is the beginning of all knowledge if we allow it to be.

POWERFUL FAITH

Have you ever watched reruns of Billy Graham preaching on television? It is incredible how simple his messages were, yet hundreds of thousands were saved through his ministry. He appeared to exert minimal effort, but he wielded immeasurable impact with his words and actions. Harvard University

Press produced a book on Graham titled *America's Pastor: Billy Graham and the Shaping of a Nation*.[4]

A close friend of mine met with Graham before his passing in his home in Montreat, North Carolina. My friend asked Graham to pray over him. Before Graham did so, he said, "Holy Spirit, we welcome You." Immediately, the supernatural presence of God filled the room, and everyone began to cry. Everything changes when the Holy Spirit rests on you in power. His presence changes atmospheres.

COURAGE IN PROCLAIMING THE GOSPEL

A little while ago, I was hosting an adult discipleship session with my friend Pat Schatzline, or as I call him, Shatz. When we had finished going over the material we had prepared on the remnant, we opened the floor up to questions. A young man asked us how he could have the courage to talk to his family and friends about Jesus. I had been prepared to give a pocketed answer and move on to the next question, but then Shatz jumped up, clapped his hands, and said, "That's easy."

He told the crowd, "If you want to receive boldness like this young man just asked for, then repeat after me." He said, "Dear God, I want to be a vessel for You. Help me to feel the love You have toward my friends and family. Help me to feel the pain You have, the hurt You have toward my friends and family who are not serving You." Then Shatz told everyone to wait for the Holy Spirit to do His work.

---

4. Grant Wacker, *America's Pastor: Billy Graham and the Shaping of a Nation* (Cambridge, MA: The Belknap Press of Harvard University Press, 2014).

About ten seconds passed before people began to cry. The gentleman who asked the question had started to bawl as well. There was no more compelling answer than allowing the Holy Spirit to do His work. As theologically sound as my pocket answer might have been, it could not have even come close to the impact made by the Holy Spirit.

A GREAT DIVERSITY OF GIFTS

On the day of Pentecost, the apostles and believers received a powerful baptism of the Holy Spirit. Finney noted, "This baptism imparted a great diversity of gifts that were used for the accomplishment of their work. It clearly included many outward things."[5] These gifts included:

+ The power of a holy life

+ The power of a self-sacrificing life

+ The power of a cross-bearing life

+ The power of great meekness, which this baptism enabled them to exhibit everywhere

+ The power of a loving enthusiasm in proclaiming the gospel

+ The power of teaching

+ The power of a loving and living faith

+ The gift of tongues

+ An increase of power to work miracles

---

5. Finney, *Power from God*, 17.

+ The gift of inspiration, or the revelation of many truths before unrecognized by them

+ The power of moral courage to proclaim the gospel and do the bidding of Christ, whatever it cost them[6]

SAVING IMPRESSIONS

When I went to Bogota, Colombia, to preach a few years back, I stayed with a man who had been praying for his daughter's salvation for years. She was a traditional Catholic, unwilling to explore her dad's faith. Still, she agreed to meet with me. We sat and had coffee together, making small talk through a translator. Eventually, she brought up her faith, seemingly out of nowhere. She said, "I am not a Christian; I am Catholic." I told her that was fine, that I had a lot of good friends who were Catholic. Then I said, "Just remember when you're looking at images of the saints and Mother Mary that they did not die for your sins. Only one man did: Jesus."

That was the simplest message I had ever given. I did not feel anything special about the words I had spoken to her, but the Holy Spirit still moved through them. Fat tears started streaming down her face, one after the other. The Lord became her Savior at that moment. And since then, she has been completely sold out, radically devoted. The Holy Spirit caused a saving impression at that moment. He did something that cannot be done by a carefully worded sermon or beautifully crafted illustration. Those things are wonderful, but they have comparatively little fruit if they do not carry God's power. Partnering with the Holy Spirit produces much more fruit.

6. Ibid.

FAVOR WITH GOD AND MAN

First Samuel 16:13 tells us that after the prophet Samuel anointed David, *"the Spirit of the Lord came powerfully upon David from that day on."* Meanwhile, the Spirit left King Saul, leaving him with *"a tormenting spirit that filled him with depression and fear"* (verse 14). Whenever that spirit troubled Saul, *"David would play the harp. Then Saul would feel better, and the tormenting spirit would go away"* (verse 23).

With the Spirit of the Lord resting upon him, David, who was just a young boy, stripped evil spirits off of the king. No counseling or medication can do what a person who has the Holy Spirit resting on them can do. *"The yoke will be destroyed because of the anointing oil"* (Isaiah 10:27 NKJV).

THE GIFT OF TONGUES AND A GIVING LIFE

Peter and John were perceived as *"uneducated, common men"* (Acts 4:13 ESV). And yet the Holy Spirit fell upon all who were listening to Peter proclaim the gospel message in Acts 10. The Jewish believers who went with Peter to the Roman officer's house *"were amazed that the gift of the Holy Spirit had been poured out on the Gentiles, too. For they heard them speaking in other tongues and praising God"* (Acts 10:45–46).

As Peter was speaking, it was as if the Holy Spirit suddenly said, "Thanks for the introduction, Peter. I'll take it from here." When the Holy Spirit rests on you in power, that partnership will produce fruit beyond your wildest imagination.

Some of the apostles received an impartation for evangelism, while others received impartations for healing, signs, wonders,

WHEN THE HOLY SPIRIT RESTS
ON YOU IN POWER,
THAT PARTNERSHIP WILL
PRODUCE FRUIT BEYOND YOUR
WILDEST IMAGINATION.

and miracles. Of course, one could argue that a few of the above manifestations could be produced without the Spirit of the Lord resting upon them. However, keep in mind that the common thread for each of those gifts is the lasting impression that they make. When people encounter someone who has received a true impartation of power flowing in their lives, the impression is so powerful that it touches their very soul.

It is important to note that when someone is endowed with power, it looks different each time. I have heard it said that there is no record of anyone receiving healing through Charles Finney's ministry, yet thousands were saved in the most miraculous ways. We can no longer be content to live or even attempt ministry without the Spirit of the Lord resting upon us in power.

Have you ever looked in the face of someone who adamantly claims to be an atheist? Or stared into the eyes of a person who truly hates everything Christianity represents? Most people have a family member who will not even entertain a conversation about Jesus. It can become easy to doubt whether these people could ever give their lives to the Lord. Without the Holy Spirit, it would surely be impossible.

We can no longer try to preach the Word of God or lead those around us to salvation leaning only on our own charisma, gifts, and talents. If the disciples who walked with Christ needed power resting on them before attempting to fulfill the Great Commission, so do we. (See Matthew 28:19–20.)

Signs of empowerment following Christians wherever they go is the blueprint of the church, the biblical example of a believer's lifestyle. (See Mark 16:17–18.) Jesus began with His twelve apostles. He *"gave them power and authority to cast out all demons and to heal all diseases"* (Luke 9:1). After they returned from their first mission on their own, Jesus looked into the crowd of His followers, selected seventy-two from among them, and gave them the authority to heal the sick and spread the message that *"the Kingdom of God is near"* (Luke 10:9).

This power to heal the sick and spread the gospel was not reserved only for the Twelve and the seventy-two. Jesus said, *"I tell you the truth, anyone who believes in me will do the same works I have done, and even greater works, because I am going to be with the Father"* (John 14:12).

One of my favorite examples of how God's power can flow in and out of those who are not in full-time ministry is found in the life of Stephen. In Acts 6:5, Stephen was one of the seven men selected by the Lord's disciples to oversee daily food distribution to widows. Scripture tells us:

Stephen, a man full of God's grace and power, performed amazing miracles and signs among the people. (Acts 6:8)

Philip, another one of the seven chosen to care for the widows, also had the power of the Holy Spirit resting upon him. On one occasion in particular, he moved from one location to another without physically traveling the distance in between. (See Acts 8:39–40.) *"God does not show favoritism"* (Romans 2:11). If God has moved through anyone—and He has—He is willing to move through you.

Leaning heavily on ourselves in an effort to produce spiritual fruit by changing lives can cause us to find out too late that all we are is *"a noisy gong or a clanging cymbal"* (1 Corinthians 13:1). Paul challenged us to *"earnestly desire the best gifts"* (1 Corinthians 12:31 NKJV). We can make a more significant impact with fewer resources, less effort, and less rambling with greater gifts.

As you read the Scriptures, you will notice that our gospel is built upon demonstration. We are not merely to love; we are to express our love to others. Notice the action words in Luke's gospel: *"Bless those who curse you. Pray for those who hurt you"* (Luke 6:28). Selective love is not love. We are commanded to *"love other believers"* (1 John 3:10) and love our enemies. (See Matthew 5:44.) True love is consistently shown. Some may ask for an impartation of power but still be unwilling to show love toward certain people in their lives.

Peter told us to be holy in every aspect of our lives—in everything we do. (See 1 Peter 1:15.) Paul told us, *"We must live decent lives for all to see"* (Romans 13:13 NLT). Paul continued his thoughts on this demonstration of our lives when he wrote:

For when we brought you the Good News, it was not only with words but also with power.   (1 Thessalonians 1:5)

Paul knew the church at Rome needed an endowment of power as well. This is why he wrote, *"For I long to see you, that I may impart to you some spiritual gift to strengthen you"* (Romans 1:11 ESV).

LEANING HEAVILY ON
OURSELVES IN AN EFFORT TO
PRODUCE SPIRITUAL FRUIT CAN
CAUSE US TO FIND OUT TOO
LATE THAT ALL WE ARE IS
"A NOISY GONG OR
A CLANGING CYMBAL."

Isaiah referred to this same power:

> *The Spirit of the Sovereign* LORD *is upon me, for the* LORD
> *has anointed me to bring good news to the poor. He has
> sent me to comfort the brokenhearted and to proclaim that
> captives will be released and prisoners will be freed.*
> (Isaiah 61:1)

Zechariah received a direct message from the Lord regarding his ministry when he said, "*Not by might, nor by power, but by my Spirit, says the* LORD *of hosts*" (Zechariah 4:6 ESV).

With such power available to any believer (see John 14:12), why are there so many powerless believers? The disciples had to wait in the upper room for over a week before the Holy Spirit came upon them. (See Acts 2.) Could it be that many of us are not willing to wait for however long it takes? Has the "ask, seek, knock" process that Jesus outlined in Matthew 7:7 become too burdensome?

Let it not be so. God's timing may not be our timing, but it *is* perfect. The following chapter discusses how to continuously contend for more of God and His presence even if it may be difficult to see the fruit.

CHAPTER 2: DISCOVERY QUESTIONS

1. How does God speak to you most often?

_____

_____

_____

_____

_____

_____

2. When the Spirit of the Lord moves through a person, "saving impressions" are made that have the power to change someone's life. Have you ever seen this happen?

_____

_____

_____

_____

_____

_____

3. How do you believe the Holy Spirit wants to partner with you?

_____

_____

_____

_____

_____

4. What thoughts come to mind when Paul challenges us to *"earnestly desire the best gifts"* (1 Corinthians 12:31 NKJV)?

_____

_____

_____

_____

_____

_____

SECTION II

HOW TO RECEIVE POWER
FROM HEAVEN

3

THE KINGDOM IS MORE THAN WORDS

The night I read Charles Finney's *Power from God* for the first time, I was rocked by how the power of God manifested so regularly in his life and ministry. I distinctly remember deciding how I would internalize the incredible testimonies of his walk with God. I was torn between two mentalities:

1. "God chose Finney; God didn't choose me to perform signs and wonders."

2. "I am not Finney, but God can still use me."

Naturally, the second option is the most attractive, so I was willing to make any sacrifice necessary to see the manifestation of the promises and power of God.

Personally, I believe that we, the followers of Christ, can over-preach the "go" message every time we talk to others about how to navigate their lives. We tell others, "Go pray," "Go read the Bible," "Go be faithful," and "Go be holy." Then we end that long-winded list of commands with, "God will be faithful."

However, "go" cannot always be our message to those who are desperate for the power of God. If you read the gospels, Jesus never said, "If you dedicate yourself to the spiritual disciplines, then I will do a miracle in your life." Instead, whenever He encountered a desperate person, He changed their life at that very moment.

Take, for instance, the Samaritan woman at the well in John 4. She had already been married to five men, and the man she was living with was not her husband. Reading between the lines, she must have been carrying a tremendous amount of hurt underneath layers of mistrust and bitterness. Yet in a moment with Jesus, the virtue of God transformed her life.

In another desperate case, a woman who had been bleeding out for twelve years without any answers from doctors felt God's virtue instantly heal her. (See Luke 8:43–48.)

As children of God, we must embrace the idea that part of our assignment is to create moments when the virtue of God will flow into someone's life and change everything. We must be

PART OF OUR ASSIGNMENT IS
TO CREATE MOMENTS WHEN
THE VIRTUE OF GOD WILL FLOW
INTO SOMEONE'S LIFE
AND CHANGE EVERYTHING.

active in this because *"the Kingdom of God is not just a lot of talk; it is living by God's power"* (1 Corinthians 4:20).

SECRET TO POWER

A. W. Tozer wrote in *The Crucified Life: How to Live Out a Deeper Christian Experience,* that a "Christian is as full of the Holy Spirit as he wants to be."[7] Countless Scriptures support such a statement, including:

Come close to God, and God will come close to you.

(James 4:8)

You will seek Me and find Me, when you search for Me with all your heart. (Jeremiah 29:13 NKJV)

How we spend our time will always reflect what is most important to us. I have heard it said that if you have more than three priorities in life, you do not have any priorities at all. Our daily schedule must prove that our appointment with the Lord is our greatest concern. Leonard Ravenhill once said, "No man is greater than his prayer life...Failing here, we fail everywhere."[8]

I am reminded of a Scripture in Isaiah that reads, *"Take no rest, all you who pray to the Lord. Give the Lord no rest until he completes his work"* (Isaiah 62:6–7). When you want to stop praying, say to yourself, "Lord, I'm too desperate to stop...I

7. A. W. Tozer, *The Crucified Life: How to Live Out a Deeper Christian Experience* (Minneapolis, MN: Bethany House Publishers, 2014), 55.
8. Leonard Ravenhill, *Why Revival Tarries* (Minneapolis, MN: Bethany House Publishers, 2010), 22.

can't stop! I won't stop until You do what only You can do." If the reason you live is to walk with God and share His love and power, pray until you get your breakthrough.

Recently, after concluding my prayer time, I decided to start over and begin my "appointment" with Him all over again as if I had never started. I told the Lord, "There is too much at stake. I must continue to pray." Charles Finney wrote, "Many faint before they have prevailed, and hence the outpouring [of power] is not received."[9]

We must not simply pray continuously. We must also pray with passion. *"The effective, fervent prayer of a righteous man avails much"* (James 5:16 NKJV). Fervency is passionate intensity. If we are going to pursue God for more of His presence, more of His power, more of His love, and more of His peace, then our energy and passion in prayer time must continually increase. It is okay to give thanks for your breakfast without energy but if you are passionate about what you are praying for, you will pray with passion. If fervency did not make a difference, Scripture would not say that it benefits us.

Fervency looks different for everyone. I usually find that I am very energetic in my prayers, flailing my arms about, pacing, kneeling, and laying with my face on the carpet. But that is not the only way. One of the most fervent prayers in the Bible looked incredibly different. Hannah was in deep anguish as she prayed for the Lord to open her womb, yet no sound came out of her moving lips. It was a quiet cry. (See 1 Samuel 1:13.) Whether you kneel, stand, pace, whisper, or cry out, the only must is fervency.

---

9. Finney, *Power from God*, 40.

WE MUST NOT
SIMPLY PRAY CONTINUOUSLY.
WE MUST ALSO PRAY
WITH PASSION.

Discussing Psalm 5:3, Charles H. Spurgeon wrote:

Do we not miss very much of the sweetness and efficacy of prayer by a want of careful meditation before it, and of hopeful expectation after it? We too often rush into the presence of God without forethought or humility… Prayer without fervency is like hunting with a dead dog, and prayer without preparation is hawking with a blind falcon. Prayer is the work of the Holy Spirit, but he works by means.[10]

Jesus challenged us in our prayer lives by saying:

Keep on asking, and you will receive what you ask for. Keep on seeking, and you will find. Keep on knocking, and the door will be opened to you. For everyone who asks, receives. Everyone who seeks, finds. And to everyone who knocks, the door will be opened.   (Matthew 7:7–8)

Often, the moment you pray, you receive your answer. However, if the request requires constant travailing, spiritual warfare, and intercession, let it be so. As Finney put it, "Let us go to the altar with all that we have and are, and let us lie there and persist in prayer until we receive the outpouring."[11] We need to roll up our sleeves and do what must be done. Remember, hunger for more of God has not been placed within your heart

---

10. Charles H. Spurgeon, *The Treasury of David*, archive.spurgeon.org/treasury/ps005.php.
11. Finney, *Power from God*, 38.

to torment you. Instead, your desire for more of God is a divine invitation to walk where only angels tread.

I remember hearing the Lord tell me one day, "Frankie, you must go to work, but stay connected with Me." My alarm had just gone off after hours of prayer, and I felt ready to go to work and tackle my day until I heard that. One of my favorite Scriptures came to mind: *"Pray in the Spirit at all times and on every occasion. Stay alert and be persistent in your prayers for all believers everywhere"* (Ephesians 6:18).

Praying should be like breathing. Staying connected to God does not mean adopting a striving mentality. Our prayer life should be one of abiding instead. Breathing is natural and effortless; we may focus on our breathing from time to time, but the question is never "to breathe or not to breathe." That should be our understanding of prayer. Smith Wigglesworth once said, "I don't often spend more than half an hour in prayer at one time, but I never go more than half an hour without praying."[12]

WALKING WITH GOD

Scripture tells us, *"Enoch walked with God"* (Genesis 5:24 NKJV).

As I study the men and women of God who experienced the manifest power of God in their lives, a common thread reveals itself: before these people ministered to others, regardless of the era in which they lived or the unique nuances of their divine assignment, they all prayed for hours.

---

12. Albert Hibbert, *Smith Wigglesworth: The Secret of His Power* (Tulsa, OK: Harrison House, 1984), 47.

OUR PRAYER LIFE SHOULD BE
ONE OF ABIDING RATHER THAN
STRIVING. PRAYING SHOULD BE
LIKE BREATHING,
NATURAL AND EFFORTLESS.

If you find that your prayer for more of His presence does not seem to be getting you anywhere after praying for some time, you have two options: you can let disappointment overtake you and quit; or you can decide to pray even more.

For example, if you are praying thirty minutes a day, pray for an hour. If you are praying for one hour already, pray for two. If you are praying for two hours, pray for three. If you are already praying for three hours, pray for four. Pray with the mindset, "I refuse to stop until I get my breakthrough."

With this in mind, it is essential to remember that *"obedience is better than sacrifice"* (1 Samuel 15:22). I know the Lord wants me to start my prayer time early in the morning. However, you may feel the Lord asking for a thirty-minute appointment at a later time. If so, give Him thirty minutes and stop caring about how much others pray. Give God what He desires. A lady in our church prays for hours upon hours regularly. Once, she prayed for thirteen hours in one day. If the amount of prayer time you are investing yields the amount of fruit you desire, you are in the sweet spot. If it is not, pray longer.

POWERFUL WORDS

The prayer of faith leads to salvation. (See Ephesians 2:8–9.) But for the power of God to consistently manifest in your life, you will need to add His Word to your prayer life. John 15:7 says, *"But if you remain in me and my words remain in you, you may ask for anything you want, and it will be granted!"* Therefore, we need His Word in us. Studying the Word of God is a two-part process. First, you want to read it and get as much of it within you as possible. Second, you want to memorize the Scriptures that build your faith.

Early on in my pursuit for more of God's presence and power in my life, as I read the Scriptures, I would write down the verses that grabbed me and add them to the list of those I wanted to know by heart. Then, I would memorize these verses by incorporating them into my daily prayers. Within a few weeks, the list had grown to pages and pages of Scriptures I had already committed to memory or would soon.

It is a powerful moment when someone asks you a question, and you can give a biblical view versus a worldly perspective. A biblical view always starts with, "The Bible says…" A worldly view always begins with, "I believe…" The more you lean on the Scriptures, the more you will witness the power they have.

Many times, I have thought, "Am I praying for nothing? Will I ever receive a greater impartation of power?" In those moments, I remind myself (and the Lord) of His words: *"He rewards those who earnestly seek him"* (Hebrews 11:6 NIV).

Any way He chooses to reward you will bless you and will be powerful. The Lord desired to use you powerfully before you had the desire to be used by Him. Let the Holy Spirit remind you that *"anyone who believes in me will do the same works I have done, and even greater works"* (John 14:12).

Numerous times, including this present moment, I have wished to be further along in the gifts of the Spirit than I am. When nearly overcome with discouragement, I read Romans 5:5: *"And this hope will not lead to disappointment. For we know how dearly God loves us, because he has given us the Holy Spirit to fill our hearts with his love."* The Bible always has the perfect words for every situation. As we long to hear from God, let us not be ignorant of what He has already said. It is in His Word that the Holy Spirit *"shows us God's deep secrets"* (1 Corinthians 2:10).

HOLINESS STILL MATTERS

First Peter 1:14–15 says, *"So you must live as God's obedient children. Don't slip back into your old ways of living to satisfy your own desires. You didn't know any better then. But now you must be holy in everything you do, just as God who chose you is holy."* Holiness is a continuous process of separating ourselves from anything ungodly.

If you want the power of the Holy Spirit to increase in your life, you need to recognize that some decisions will need to be made in your personal life. All too often, we want blessings but are unwilling to make the necessary sacrifices. Paul wrote:

> *Now in a great house there are not only vessels of gold and silver but also of wood and clay, some for honorable use, some for dishonorable. Therefore, if anyone cleanses himself from what is dishonorable, he will be a vessel for honorable use, set apart as holy, useful to the master of the house, ready for every good work.* (2 Timothy 2:20–21 ESV)

Many want to believe that an honorable use in the kingdom of God is possible without any participation or sacrifice on their

THE BIBLE ALWAYS HAS THE PERFECT WORDS FOR EVERY SITUATION. AS WE LONG TO HEAR FROM GOD, LET US NOT BE IGNORANT OF WHAT HE HAS ALREADY SAID.

part. The people I have heard say such things do not display the Holy Spirit's power in their lives. Let me be clear:

> *God the Father knew you and chose you long ago, and his Spirit has made you holy. As a result, you have obeyed him and have been cleansed by the blood of Jesus Christ.*
>
> (1 Peter 1:2)

Each member of the Trinity has a role in your life. However, you, too, have a part to play. Did you catch that ever-so-important phrase, *"As a result, you have obeyed him"*? If you want to be a vessel God pours His power through, you must ask your Comforter, the Holy Spirit, to teach you what to do and what not to do. (See John 14:26.)

Maybe He will remind you of someone you must forgive. Perhaps He will bring to your remembrance a secret sin pattern that must be laid on the altar before you can begin asking for more extraordinary things. Sin does not only consist of the *big* things like lust, theft, and violence. Sin can also appear in more mundane ways.

Scripture says, *"But among you there must not be even a hint of sexual immorality, or of any kind of impurity, or of greed, because these are improper for God's holy people"* (Ephesians 5:3 NIV). Did you catch the phrase, *"There must not be even a hint of sexual immorality"*? It is a given that this means that we must stay away from pornography and sex outside of marriage. But let us also consider how we dress. In today's world, for the men who work out at a gym, there are plenty of flattering T-shirts that will show off their efforts. Ladies, chances are you look in the mirror before you leave the house. I would challenge you to ask your-self, "Is there even a hint of sexuality in how I'm dressed?" If you are not sure, ask the Holy Spirit. Say, "Holy Spirit, are You okay with this outfit?" I trust that He will answer you. Do you trust yourself to obey Him?

More than just our actions must be submitted to the Holy Spirit's work in us. Our emotions must also be submitted.

Many years ago, a massive crowd of pro-life Christians cam-paigned against legalized abortion on the streets of Washington, D.C. On the same day, on the other side of the road, pro-choice supporters were campaigning for legalized abortion. These two opposing groups shouted at each other with tremendous, unbri-dled amounts of anger. People would cross the street to yell in the faces of the strangers they ideologically opposed. Though I am wholeheartedly against legalized abortion, I could not help but wonder, "If Jesus was here, is this how He would act?" I do not think so.

Because we belong to the day, we must live decent lives for all to see. Don't participate in the darkness of wild parties and drunkenness, or in sexual promiscuity and immoral living, or in quarreling and jealousy. (Romans 13:13)

There is no asterisk telling us that "quarreling" is fine under certain circumstances. Isaiah prophesied that Jesus would *"not shout or raise his voice in public"* (Isaiah 42:2). We must aim to reflect Jesus in all things. It is not just what we do that matters. The intent, the heart, behind our actions must also be submit-ted to His will. Those who aim to be like Jesus must also aim not to slander anyone. (See Proverbs 20:19.) We cannot get on our knees and ask for our lips to be an instrument of His use (see Romans 6:13) and then use those very same lips to condemn or curse one another.

When you sit down with a true man or woman of God, you will not hear them speak ill of anyone. Ever. Instead, you will notice a distinct humility about them, as if they truly think of others as better than themselves. (See Philippians 2:3.) As Christians, we should carry ourselves differently.

An example of the Holy Spirit raising the standard for holiness in my life happened while talking to a friend on the phone about a minister I had never met. When I got off the phone, I felt a great conviction over how I spoke. I knew I had to apologize to my friend immediately, so I called them back and did just that. And I said to the Lord, "I will never speak of anyone like that again." In my spirit, I felt Him say, "I want more than that. I want you to change the subject the next time anyone speaks of someone's sin, fault, or shortcoming from this moment forward."

All of us want to hear the Spirit of the Lord whisper a word of knowledge, a word of wisdom, or a word of prophecy to us. However, it is important to note that our ability to receive those words will not outpace our ability to listen and respond to the words of admonition He gives.

If you ask God to bless you, you must be willing to lay everything the Holy Spirit brings to your remembrance on the altar. David, a man after God's own heart, wrote:

OUR ABILITY TO RECEIVE A WORD OF KNOWLEDGE, WISDOM, OR PROPHECY WILL NOT OUTPACE OUR ABILITY TO LISTEN AND RESPOND TO THE LORD'S WORDS OF ADMONITION.

*Every morning you'll hear me at it again. Every morning I
lay out the pieces of my life on your altar and watch for fire
to descend.* (Psalm 5:3 MSG)

Even when we are fully submitted to God and His commands, it is highly doubtful that we will ever use the gifts with perfection. The possibility of failure will always exist. However, if we lead with humility, taking a misstep will not be as painful. I have mentioned this before, but it is worth repeating: from the outset, before you give a word to someone, if you say something along the lines of, "If I have heard the Lord correctly," the person you are talking to will most likely have grace toward you if you are wrong.

A WORD THAT WAS WORTH THE RISK

I was twenty-one years old and living in Rockford, Illinois, when my mother-in-the-Lord, Jeanne Mayo, told me, "Frankie, I met a girl while ministering in Vancouver, Canada. If I heard the Lord correctly, He said, 'This girl is for Frankie.'" She was not 100 percent certain that she was right. For that matter, I was 100 percent sure that she was wrong. But it was worth the risk! Jeanne flew the girl to Rockford a few months later. Her name was Allie. The moment I met her; I knew she was the one for me. Three days later, we were dating. A year and a half later, we were married. Today, we have three children, two dogs, and eight chickens to boot.

If Jeanne had been wrong, I would have simply said, "Thanks for thinking of me." Life moves on. Either way, I would have been thankful that she took the risk. Because she heard right,

I am even more grateful that Jeanne decided to operate in her God-given gift and speak into my life. You never know what impact your obedience can have on another's life.

OBEY WHEN YOU'RE LED TO PRAY

Even if your obedience does not yield the expected fruit, there is still value in it.

Once when I was in a movie theater, I could not help but be distracted by an older gentleman on a breathing machine sitting behind me. I decided to meet with him after the movie so that I could pray for him. When I walked out into the hallway at the end of the film, I lingered near the doors waiting for him to exit. When he did, I walked up to him and said, "Hello, I'm Frankie. I've seen Jesus heal a lot of people, and I believe He will heal you. Can I pray for you?" He did not want me to pray for him, but he still said, "Sure. Go for it."

I laid my hands on his chest as he walked. He did not stop walking the entire time I prayed. He even got in his car with one of my hands still on his chest. I only stopped praying when he drove away. I felt so dumb, knowing that he left without a single manifestation of healing. However, I did not let that feeling stop me the next time I felt led to pray for someone. I have since concluded that I would rather walk away having tried than walk away feeling the regret of not trying at all. After all, experience is what you get when you do not get what you want. Without risk-taking, it is doubtful that we will ever get to partner with Jesus in miraculous ways.

You may never know whether you have received an impartation of power or a gift until you are willing to take the risk and step out in faith. I have studied men and women of God who, throughout history, moved mightily in the gifts of the Spirit. To the best of my remembrance, not one of them knew they had been empowered until they took action. Likewise, you will never be 100 percent sure of whether you have a prophetic word, a word of knowledge, or a word of wisdom until you open your mouth and say something.

RECEIVING A WORD OF KNOWLEDGE

I recall vividly being in Brazil with Dr. Randy Clark. As he was closing his message during one service, Marcus, one of his assistants, came over to me and said, "Dr. Randy wants you to come onto the platform." I asked him why. I thought it was very odd for him to ask me to join him. I was sitting in the front row to learn. What purpose could I have fulfilled on the stage? Still, I walked onto the stage and stood next to the drums. Marcus stood next to me, so I asked him why I had been asked to come up. He told me, "At this time of the service, Dr. Randy always goes for healing, so he's probably going to ask you to give a word of knowledge identifying someone in the audience the Lord wants to heal."

I looked squarely into Marcus's eyes and said, "I've never had a word of knowledge, and I certainly do not have one right now." He started laughing as if I was joking. I was not. Not even close. I did not join in as he laughed; I just stared at him. Marcus had been with Dr. Clark for so long that receiving a word of knowledge had become second nature to him. Not for me. Marcus eventually saw that I was serious, so he let me return to my seat.

IF YOU WANT TO OPERATE IN
THE GIFTS, YOU HAVE TO STEP
OUT AND TAKE A RISK. FIND
COMFORT IN THE FACT THAT
PETER AND JOHN ALSO HAD TO
PRAY FOR BOLDNESS.

When I returned to the hotel after service, I started to reread Dr. Clark's book *Words of Knowledge*.[13] I had thumbed through it before, but at that moment, I was desperate. When I saw Dr. Clark the following day, I said, "I reread your book last night. How do I know the impression I'm having is from God and not me?" He enjoyed giving me the answer much more than I wanted to hear it. He said, "You won't know until you say it. If you're right, it was God. If you're wrong, it wasn't." Then he smiled. I wanted him to say something that would give me full assurance that my impression was from God. But there is no such thing.

I once heard Heidi Baker, a Christian missionary and the CEO of Iris Global, who has countless stories of miracles, say that everything about your life does not change simply because you got "zapped" in Toronto or Brownsville. There is a process that must be undergone—the process of learning how to operate in the spiritual gifts.

If you want to operate in the gifts, you have to step out and take a risk. There is no getting around it. Todd White, a senior pastor of Lifestyle Christian Church, known for seeing healings while praying for people on the streets and in grocery stores, says he prayed for over a thousand people in public before one person received their healing.[14] Now, people are healed all the time when he prays for them.

---

13. Randy Clark, *Words of Knowledge* (Mechanicsburg, PA: Global Awakening, 2012).
14. Nicholas C. Stern, "Recovering addict who found new path of healing in Christianity to speak in Frederick," *The Frederick News-Post*, January 21, 2012, updated March 11, 2016, www.fredericknewspost.com/archive/recovering-addict-who-found-new-path-of-healing-in-christianity-to-speak-in-frederick/article_5155a5f9-e72b-5f7a-88d5-6337c7d263cd.html.

I have heard it said, "You spell faith, R-I-S-K." You may think you do not have the boldness to step out if you are not 100 percent sure that Jesus will back you up. Find comfort in the fact that Peter and John felt the same way. In Acts 4:29, they said, "*And now, O Lord, hear their threats, and give us, your servants, great boldness in preaching your word.*" The disciples were afraid and cried out for courage. In Acts 14:3, they received courage and were "*preaching boldly about the grace of the Lord. And the Lord proved their message was true by giving them power to do miraculous signs and wonders.*" The Lord answered their request; He will answer yours as well.

Your confidence will grow as you see success since that will come from taking risks, stepping out, and using the gifts you are compelled to use. Imagine swinging on a rope tied to a tree branch hanging over the water. The first thing you want to do is tug on the rope to ensure it will not fall apart mid-swing. You may even let it hold some of your weight to get a feel for the rope's strength. Ultimately though, you will never know whether the rope is strong enough to carry you unless you hold tight to it and jump. As soon as you do that, you will know whether the rope is as safe as it appeared. Once you have allowed the rope to swing you around, you will no longer be nervous; the rope swing will become fun. The next time you grab that rope, you will not even think about its strength; you will just grab on and let it take you for a ride.

The same is true of your confidence in your ability to operate in the spiritual gifts. Once you step out a few times, though there might always be an element of nervousness, you will see that the fruit is worth the risk.

If you are still struggling with taking the plunge, go and be a student. In today's day and age, anyone can mentor you if you are willing. There are countless books, YouTube videos, articles, and other sources to help you. See yourself as a lifelong learner. Continually study. I have learned more by watching people I admire than I can measure. I once heard it said, "The years will teach what the days never will." Go to conferences, mission trips, and church services. Do whatever you have to do to study those who are already doing what you hope to do one day.

So often, when we see someone who has a gift we admire, we let ourselves become too distracted by the off-putting things we see in their ministry. I would suggest diving in regardless, even if it is with caution. I remember the Lord telling me once, "Frankie, you'll never learn from the people you're judging." It is also important to recognize that when we get to heaven, we may find out that what we were sure of, we were completely wrong about. So we should humble ourselves and be willing to learn.

CHAPTER 3: DISCOVERY QUESTIONS

1. Scriptures speak of the power of *"effective, fervent prayer"* (James 5:16 NKJV). What is the difference between a fervent prayer and a non-fervent prayer?

_____

_____

_____

_____

_____

2. How could you create a moment for God's love and power to flow through you?

_____

_____

_____

_____

_____

3. This chapter referenced something Smith Wigglesworth once said: "I don't often spend more than a half an hour in prayer at one time, but I never go more than half an hour without praying." What kind of mindset would you need to have such a prayer life?

_____

_____

_____

_____

_____

_____

4. How would you define holiness?

_____

_____

_____

_____

_____

_____

4

IMPARTATION IS ESSENTIAL

We will always need more of God's power in our lives. There comes a point in every pastor's ministry when their church cannot continue as usual. For me, it was when our Sunday attendance numbers and incredible family programming were no longer enough. I was desperate to see God move in a New Testament way, with demonstrations of power that would make people whole through healing and restoration.

For a year and a half, I prayed for hours, almost daily, for an impartation of power. I searched the Internet for a pastor who had a thriving church and demonstrated the Holy Spirit's power. At the time, the only person I could find was Pastor Bill Johnson of Bethel Church in Redding, California. I watched YouTube clips of him repeatedly looking to see how the Holy Spirit flowed through him. Thousands were receiving healing in his church. The wonderful thing was that most of the healings came through the saints who attended his church, not through him.

Toward the end of 2018, a name I did not recognize popped up on my YouTube feed. In the "Recommended for You" section was a video titled, "Randy Clark Interviews Bill Johnson."[15] I clicked on the video and watched Pastor Bill Johnson and Dr. Clark chat with one another, trading healing testimonies as casually as I would talk about a football game with a friend. I was utterly blown away by the regularity of the miraculous in their lives. As I continued to watch Dr. Clark in conversation, I had this thought: "Reach out to him. He can help you."

I began searching to find out who he was. I discovered that he is not a pastor. Instead, he has a ministry called Global Awakening. I called the ministry and asked for Dr. Clark's assistant. On the other line, all I heard was the voice mail, so I left a message.

"Hello," I said. "My name is Frankie Mazzapica. I'm a pastor in The Woodlands, Texas. I'm calling to request one hour of Dr.

---

15. Praying Medic, "Randy Clark Interviews Bill Johnson," November 2010, vimeo.com/78413137?embedded=true&source=video_title&owner=9347046.

Clark's time. I will fly anywhere in the country to meet him at any time. I'll be prepared with questions written down. I promise to start on time and end on time."

A few days later, his administrative assistant called and told me that he would be speaking at a conference in Virginia the following month. Between sessions, he would meet with me.

When the day arrived, I had twenty questions ready. We got through all of them, but it was his answer to the first question that deeply affected me. Sitting across from Dr. Clark in the green room, I asked, "Is there a difference between being baptized in the Holy Spirit and receiving an endowment of power?" He smiled and said, "Yes." At that point, I was tempted to stand and walk out. What he had just said blew my entire traditional Pentecostal theology to smithereens. I was raised to believe that if you received the baptism of the Holy Spirit with the evidence of speaking in tongues, you had it all.

Shortly after that, I asked, "How does one receive an impartation of power?" I had assumed I knew the answer because I have always been a huge believer in the power of prayer. Dr. Clark threw me off when he said, "You need to come with me to Brazil." I told him that I appreciated the invitation, but I was not interested in taking a trip halfway around the world to see miracles that would not translate to America. He assured me that the miracles would transfer over. I just looked at him after that. He wore a kind, extremely confident smile. My face was full of unbelief. But I was hungry and desperate, so I agreed to meet him in Brazil later in the year.

WHAT DR. RANDY CLARK SAID
BLEW MY ENTIRE TRADITIONAL
PENTECOSTAL THEOLOGY
TO SMITHEREENS.

AN INTRODUCTION GOES AWRY

Two weeks before leaving for Brazil, I became aware of Elijah Rising, a nonprofit ministry that brings awareness to and combats sex trafficking. We invited the director, a thirty-year-old young lady named Micah Gamboa, to come to Celebration Church for an interview in front of our congregation. She walked onto our platform and took a seat at the table we had set up. I started with a general introductory question. I said, "Tell Celebration Church a little bit about yourself." She said, "Well, first, I would like to say thank you so much for inviting me."

Then her eyes rolled back, and she began to slide out of her chair. At first, I thought she was having a seizure. I grabbed her before she could fall and gently laid her on the floor, encouraging her to relax and telling her that everything was and would be okay. But then she stopped breathing. My hands were still behind her head as I saw the life leave her eyes. Later, I found out she went into full cardiac arrest. Her lungs were not working; there was no brain function. Her heart was not beating.

Two people rushed up to the platform: a lady in our congregation who's an emergency room physician and a gentleman who had served two tours in Afghanistan. Both were trained in cardiopulmonary resuscitation and performed CPR on Micah until the paramedics arrived. While the physician and the veteran worked, our congregation prayed out in the hallway.

About fifteen minutes later, an ambulance showed up and started hooking Micah up to all kinds of machines. I did not know what was happening, but I did recognize the eerie, monotone sound that meant her heart was still not beating. She had been dead for fifteen minutes on our stage.

Then, suddenly, her heart began to beat again. The paramedics placed her on a stretcher, wheeled her out of the building, and rushed her to the hospital. She still had no brain or lung activity when she left. I heard later that she was in a coma. A good friend who was a doctor said that most people who go into full cardiac arrest are dead by the time they reach the hospital. Micah was not. That same friend told me that I should still prepare myself. He said he did not know what the lasting effects would be, but she would never be the same again.

I asked, "What if she is okay? What if she is perfect as if nothing ever happened?"

He said, "That is not going to happen. But on the chance it does, I don't want to stand close to you or Celebration Church because lightning has struck. God is doing something."

A MIRACULOUS RECOVERY

Micah woke herself up out of her coma less than forty-eight hours after being checked into the hospital. As soon as I was allowed, I went to see her. She looked at me and said, "Dude, I'm so sorry I messed up your service, man."

I was in total shock. She was completely fine! The next day, she walked out of the hospital. Only God could have brought her through that. The only thing she could not remember was the morning of the incident.

In hindsight, what happened to Micah Gamboa unlocked a floodgate of miracles in our church. Now I jokingly tell her and her husband David, "Thanks for taking one for the team."

Two weeks after Micah's medical miracle, I arrived in Brazil to meet up with Dr. Clark. At my first opportunity, I sat down with him over a cup of espresso and said, "I don't expect you to have an answer, but I must ask you anyway. Why did Micah Gamboa, a perfectly healthy young woman with no medical history, die in our church on our stage? Am I supposed to chalk it up to coincidence?"

His reply changed my life. He said, "I don't know why she died that day. But I do know that you saw someone die and come back to life. When you have the faith to see someone go from dead to living, there's not a lot you can't believe God for. I believe you're called to heal the sick." He was so confident when he said that. I could tell he genuinely meant what he said, which caused me to believe it as well.

Throughout the week, I was one of Dr. Clark's many prayer partners, the perfect place to be if God was ever going to flow through me and heal someone miraculously on that trip. The first person I prayed for was a man with fractured bones in his foot. While I was praying for him, he started telling me that his ankle felt hot. I thought, *No way. I'm not even praying that hard. I've only said two sentences.* I continued to pray, and then he grabbed me and hugged me. He was so thankful! I could not match his excitement because I thought he had to be lying. I had barely prayed!

DR. CLARK TOLD ME, "WHEN YOU HAVE THE FAITH TO SEE SOMEONE GO FROM DEAD TO LIVING, THERE'S NOT A LOT YOU CAN'T BELIEVE GOD FOR."

Something very similar happened when I prayed for the next person. They were overjoyed with their healing. I looked at them, baffled, because I still could not believe that someone had been healed through my prayer. Finally, I went to the third person who, if I remember correctly, wanted prayer for a hurt shoulder. When the shoulder was healed, you could see the excitement written on their face. I thought, *Either they never had the pain to begin with, or they were never truly healed.* By the end of the week, between fourteen and sixteen people I had prayed for were healed. In the craziness of that trip, I was unable to recall the exact number, but my faith increased regardless.

IMPARTATION IS REAL

When I went home after Brazil, Dr. Clark told me to pray over each one of Celebration Church's prayer partners. The result has been nothing short of amazing. The power of Jesus flows through them and me regularly. Every time we go for healing in our services, people get healed. Anytime I have traveled to another church to minister, people get healed.

Impartations are a very real thing. As I mentioned earlier, I use impartation and endowment interchangeably. For this book's context, the working definition of each is the giving and receiving of spiritual gifts, blessings, healing, and baptism in the Holy Spirit for the building up of the church and the work of the ministry. An impartation of power is essential for fulfilling our divine assignment.

For we are not fighting against flesh-and-blood enemies,
but against evil rulers and authorities of the unseen world,

against mighty powers in this dark world, and against evil spirits in the heavenly places. (Ephesians 6:12)

You and I are fighting supernatural battles. Therefore, we require supernatural weapons and spiritual skills to wage war effectively.

This is why I believe that both lay and full-time ministers are working too hard without an impartation of power. Furthermore, they are producing only a fraction of the fruit they otherwise could.

In my opinion, burnout happens when we lean on our own strength too much. I am not saying the practical side of ministry is a breeze. I come home exhausted all the time from all-day strategy or counseling meetings that physically and mentally tax me. Nevertheless, ministry should be a life-giving experience. It gives us front-row seats to Jesus's miraculous work. Paul wrote:

I came to you in weakness—timid and trembling. And my message and my preaching were very plain. Rather than using clever and persuasive speeches, I relied only on the power of the Holy Spirit. (1 Corinthians 2:3–4)

As A. W. Tozer once said, "It's not the load that breaks you down; it's the way you carry it."

God can place His power in or upon anyone, anytime and any way He wants. The Holy Spirit can do something for the first time—anytime. We must be careful not to limit our

THE GIVING AND RECEIVING OF SPIRITUAL GIFTS, BLESSINGS, HEALING, AND BAPTISM IN THE HOLY SPIRIT IS ESSENTIAL FOR THE BUILDING UP OF THE CHURCH AND THE WORK OF THE MINISTRY.

understanding of impartation to what we ourselves have heard about or seen.

Even so, we still should study the biblical examples of impartation. Though the Holy Spirit can do something new at any point in time, the new thing will not contradict the old. For example, in Acts 10:44–46, at Cornelius's house, God's power moved without the laying on of hands. However, in Acts 19:6, an impartation was accompanied by the laying on of hands with tongues and prophecy.

TWO WAYS TO RECEIVE AN IMPARTATION

With these examples in mind, the two ways of receiving an impartation that I am most familiar with are:

1. Directly from Jesus Christ Himself

2. Coming from Jesus Christ through one person onto another

First, let us discuss impartations received directly from Jesus. John the Baptist told us:

> *Someone is coming soon who is greater than I am—so much greater that I'm not even worthy to be his slave and untie the straps of his sandals. He will baptize you with the Holy Spirit and with fire.* (Luke 3:16)

Jesus is the one who baptizes us in the Spirit. We know that the Spirit of God is often represented with fire—from the pillar of fire in the desert to the consuming fire in the temple to the

WE MUST BE CAREFUL NOT TO
LIMIT OUR UNDERSTANDING
OF IMPARTATION TO WHAT
WE OURSELVES HAVE HEARD
ABOUT OR SEEN.

tongues of fire in the upper room. (See Exodus 13:21, 1 Kings 18:38, and Acts 2:3, respectively.)

Jesus wants to baptize you in the Spirit. After John the Baptist preached his message of baptism, God anointed Jesus *"with the Holy Spirit and with power"* (Acts 10:38). Jesus later said, *"As the Father has sent me, so I am sending you"* (John 20:21).

Jesus also told us:

> I tell you the truth, anyone who believes in me will do the same works I have done, and even greater works, because I am going to be with the Father.   (John 14:12)

If you have never been baptized in the Holy Spirit, just ask for it. Jesus said, *"So if you sinful people know how to give good gifts to your children, how much more will your heavenly Father give the Holy Spirit to those who ask him"* (Luke 11:13).

Second, let us discuss impartations received through fellow believers. Jesus will often use people as vessels to pour out more of His love, Spirit, and power into others. For example, in his letter to Rome, Paul wrote, *"For I long to see you, that I may impart to you some spiritual gift to strengthen you"* (Romans 1:11 ESV). Timothy received an impartation through prophecy when the elders laid their hands upon him. (See 1 Timothy 4:14.) He also received an impartation from Paul when Paul laid hands on him. (See 2 Timothy 1:6.)

There are many Old Testament examples of God blessing people when hands were laid upon them, my favorite being when Jacob was willing to lie, cheat, and steal to get the blessing intended for his twin brother Esau. (See Genesis 27.) Your next impartation could just as easily come through the laying on of hands as it could from God Himself.

In the first chapter of this book, I shared a moment in Costa Rica in which a few local residents were healed as they prayed for one another. However, I never prayed for any of them to receive an impartation for healing. I just told them to pray for one another with short, commanding prayers in the name of Jesus. Everyone prayed for was healed in the name of Jesus!

I called Dr. Clark afterward and asked, "How did that happen? Was there an impartation from you to me, to them?" He told me that this was a possibility but he was not sure.

"I believe the locals, maybe for the first time in their life, had permission to step out in faith and pray for someone," Dr. Clark said. "I believe the power of a commanding prayer in Jesus's name caused miracles to happen. I think believers praying for one another is the church's blueprint, and God blessed what He saw."

Here is the takeaway: it is of great importance to get into an environment where God's power is manifesting. If you are standing in the middle of supernatural activity, something beyond your understanding is happening. Your experience will provoke your faith. The more faith you possess, the more of God you will experience.

If God has done something for anyone and you desire the same, ask for it. In Scripture, we see that impartations can also come through dreams. As a point of reference, "*The LORD*

IF YOU ARE STANDING IN THE MIDDLE OF SUPERNATURAL ACTIVITY, SOMETHING BEYOND YOUR UNDERSTANDING IS HAPPENING. YOUR EXPERIENCE WILL PROVOKE YOUR FAITH.

appeared to Solomon in a dream, and God said, 'What do you want? Ask, and I will give it to you!'" (1 Kings 3:5). Solomon answered:

> *Give me an understanding heart so that I can govern your people well and know the difference between right and wrong.*   (Verse 9)

The Lord was pleased with Solomon's request for wisdom and therefore granted it. (See 1 Kings 3:10–12.) Solomon loved the Lord, obeyed the Law, and worshipped God. This was enough for the Lord to come to him in a dream and give him an impartation of wisdom that had never been seen before and has never been seen since.

Does your heart desire to love the Lord, obey His commands, and worship? If so, you are a candidate for an impartation of a supernatural gift from our heavenly Father. As I read the Scriptures, I constantly remind myself that these men and women were as human as I am. Therefore, what they reached out to God for—or what He reached down and offered to them—is not only possible but within the character and nature of a good, good Father.

CHAPTER 4: DISCOVERY QUESTIONS

1. Jesus told His disciples to wait to be *"endued with power from on high"* (Luke 24:49 NKJV) before they continued their ministry. Do you believe receiving an endowment or impartation of power is still important today?

_____

_____

_____

_____

_____

2. What are the two ways someone could receive an impartation of power?

_____

_____

_____

_____

_____

3. Did you know that all believers can receive an impartation of power?

_____

_____

_____

_____

_____

4. An impartation of power allows a believer to share God's love and power to leave a lasting impression that completely changes one's life. Give some examples of how you would imagine this could happen.

_____

_____

_____

_____

_____

SECTION III

BURNING QUESTIONS AND MINISTRY IN THE LAST DAYS

5

ELEPHANTS IN THE ROOM

Anytime someone is around the supernatural, there are always questions. In all honesty, there is a mountain of skepticism. The apostle Paul knew this would be the case, so he warned us not to operate in the gift of speaking in tongues when unbelievers are in the room because *"they will think you are crazy"* (1 Corinthians 14:23).

During the worship portion of our services, I speak in tongues at least 50 percent of the time because I believe speaking in tongues strengthens our spirits. (See 1 Corinthians 14:4.) However, I speak in a whisper because I know that there are unbelievers or people around me who do not understand the gift of tongues.

Many believers take great offense when they are asked not to speak in tongues aloud in church. When I get pushed into a corner by these people, I usually ask them, "When was the last time you brought an unbeliever to church?" In nearly every case, it has been years since they brought someone to worship with them. When church is all about us, it is easy to care less about others. When church is all about others, we care less about ourselves.

However, this does not mean all of our questions will go away. In this chapter, I will do my best to address the elephants in the room.

BAPTISM IN THE HOLY SPIRIT

Growing up a traditional Pentecostal, I believed speaking in tongues was the only evidence of being Spirit-filled. Therefore, it was revelatory when I noticed that not everyone in the Bible who was baptized in the Spirit spoke in tongues. (See Acts 2:4; compare Acts 4:31.) History makes no mention of whether people like Billy Graham, Mother Teresa, John Wesley, Charles Finney, George Whitefield, or John G. Lake ever spoke in tongues.[16] Yet the power displayed in their lives makes it clear: that power came from on high, so speaking in tongues cannot be the only evidence of a Holy Spirit baptism.

---

16. Clark, *There Is More!*, 222.

Despite this, everyone wants to know if there is proof of being filled with the Holy Spirit. The only evidence of being filled with the Holy Spirit is the fruit that manifests in your life. Dr. Randy Clark communicated this so well in his book *There Is More!* He wrote, "It is not enough to have received a baptism in the Holy Spirit; we must continue being filled with the Spirit."[17]

PROPHECY

Prophecy is speaking on behalf of God. There are many different types of prophets in the Bible. Some, like Ezekiel, received prophetic words through dreams. (See Ezekiel 37.) Others received words through visions, like Peter and John. (See Acts 10; Revelation.) Some biblical prophetic ministries operated in the sphere of knowledge (see 1 Samuel 9) and prophetic demonstrations (see Ezekiel 4–5). Others prophesied the future when they spoke. (See Acts 21:11.) Elisha and Elijah prophesied using signs and wonders. (See 1 Kings.) Moses prophesied as he was leading and teaching. (See Deuteronomy 18:15, 34:10.) Finally, some men of God, like Micaiah, were known to give gloomy prophecies but were always right. (See 2 Chronicles 18.)

Scripture tells us:

Beloved, do not believe every spirit, but test the spirits to see whether they are from God, for many false prophets have gone out into the world. (1 John 4:1 ESV)

---

17. Ibid., 221.

THE ONLY EVIDENCE OF BEING
FILLED WITH THE HOLY SPIRIT
IS THE FRUIT THAT MANIFESTS
IN YOUR LIFE.

Prophecies should be tested by cross-reference with the Word of God. Jesus is the living Word (see John 1:1), and the Scriptures are the inspired Word of God. (See 2 Timothy 3:16.) Therefore, God will never say anything that contradicts the Scriptures.

Many people have told me that God told them it was okay to do something that is clearly against the Word of God. I have also heard supposedly prophetic words that do not sound anything like the character of God. This is why all prophecies must be tested through the lens of the Scriptures. We must also check to see whether the prophetic word resonates with the Holy Spirit within us.

I have heard several positive words spoken over me that were not true. As exciting as these words were to my flesh, I knew that what the people were saying was something *they* wanted to happen, not something God said would happen. I have also had people prophesy some pretty ugly things to me, and the Spirit within me instantly told me to reject what I heard. If you are ever unsure, go to a spiritual leader in your life and allow them to help you sort through the prophecy.

Sadly, many who claim to hear from God are lying. Social media and the Internet give these people a platform, enabling them to deceive millions. If someone claims they have heard from God and the opportunity for fulfillment has passed, they did *not* hear from God. If they continue to be wrong, someone needs to tell them to stop claiming that they have heard from God.

When someone is continuously wrong, they are hurting the church, not helping it. Jesus warned against false teachers when He told the disciples:

> *Don't let anyone mislead you, for many will come in my name, claiming, "I am the Messiah." They will deceive many.*
>
> (Matthew 24:4–5)

Paul echoed Jesus's words when he wrote to Timothy:

> *For a time is coming when people will no longer listen to sound and wholesome teaching. They will follow their own desires and will look for teachers who will tell them whatever their itching ears want to hear. They will reject the truth and chase after myths.* (2 Timothy 4:3–4)

I admit that false prophets anger me a great deal. Christianity takes a black eye every time a false prophecy goes public. And these false prophets rarely, if ever, apologize; they just let some time pass and then start telling people that they have heard from the Lord once again. Despite my strong feelings, each of us must honor the Scriptures more than we despise falsehood. The Bible says, *"Do not scoff at prophecies, but test everything that is said"* (1 Thessalonians 5:20–21). We will not be judged by what men say; we will be judged by how we respond.

If you want to operate in the prophetic but do not know how to get started, always remember that being humble and encouraging someone with Scripture is still operating in the gift of prophecy. Prophecies are meant to strengthen, encourage, and comfort. (See 1 Corinthians 14:3.) Therefore, if you speak the blessings and the promises found in Scripture into people's lives, you are sure to be echoing the heart of God. Other thoughts or impressions may come to your mind beyond what you originally planned to say as you bless people. That is prophecy. Simply remember to lead with love and lead with humility. Know the Word, and the Lord will bless you.

BELIEVING FOR HEALING

The healing ministry will keep you humble. You either learn humility, or you stop going for healing. It is that simple. If you say you have a word of knowledge that someone is about to get healed, and it does not happen, you will feel beads of sweat running down your back. After making many mistakes, one lesson I learned is to say something up-front, which takes all the pressure off me. Regularly, I say from the platform, "It feels like my words of knowledge regarding immediate healing are 70 percent accurate. The other 30 percent of the time, I'm off."

Letting people know that I can be wrong about hearing from God makes them much more gracious when something does not go as hoped. Additionally, the more humble and honest I am, the more accurate I am in the gifts. Jesus shows His lovingkindness in those situations by moving mightily, fulfilling His promise to show favor to the humble. (See James 4:6.)

If you have not thought this to yourself, you have probably heard it asked, "How do we know if the person who is testifying of their healing was healed?" As I shared earlier, I have wondered that myself. I have concluded that it is important to ask

BEING HUMBLE AND
ENCOURAGING SOMEONE WITH
SCRIPTURE IS STILL OPERATING
IN THE GIFT OF PROPHECY.

yourself whether it sounds like the newly healed person is lying. If they do not sound like they are lying, why not celebrate with them? You may not know them, but they are happy, so be happy with them.

We should not position ourselves as a judge. That seat is not for us. As the Scriptures say, *"The standard you use in judging is the standard by which you will be judged"* (Matthew 7:2). Even so, it can still be difficult to push aside doubts when listening to the healing testimonies of people with little credibility. If they are lying but happy, you can still be happy with them. That does not mean that you need to ignore what you see. Instead, I would encourage you to say to the Lord, "Jesus, I want what I see to be true. Help my unbelief." The Holy Spirit can give you complete assurance that what you see and hear is true. (See 1 Thessalonians 1:5.) Healings follow those who believe (see Mark 16:17–18), but if what you see is not what He is doing, He will lead you to where He is moving.

There are times when a person receives healing, and then the sickness or illness, whatever it was, returns. Do not doubt that healing has happened. Scripture explains what happens in cases like these.

> *When an unclean spirit goes out of a man, he goes through dry places, seeking rest, and finds none. Then he says, "I will return to my house from which I came."*
> (Matthew 12:43–44 NKJV)

These unclean spirits are like boomerangs. You cast them out, and then they circle back around. It is up to the person who received their healing to continue to claim their healing and use their God-given authority to rebuke the evil spirit. Former British Prime Minister Margaret Thatcher memorably said, "You may have to fight a battle more than once to win it."

UNANSWERED PRAYERS

Before our growth spurt, when Celebration Church was only a few years old, Allie and I could have a close relationship with nearly everyone in our church. During that time, a forty-one-year-old single mother named Lonna, who was very dear to us, discovered she had stage four lung cancer. She was young, vibrant, and healthy. She had never touched a cigarette in her life.

Her daughter Hallie was eleven years old with long brown hair, big brown eyes, and thick eyebrows. She was one of the sweetest, most tenderhearted individuals I had ever met. At her young age, she looked up at me with her thick-framed glasses near the tip of her nose and said, "Pastor Frankie, I'm not worried. I know Jesus will heal her."

Lonna started chemotherapy only days after her diagnosis. Her youthful skin quickly turned yellow, her blue eyes grew heavy, and her thick brown hair thinned out. Nevertheless, I was full of faith. I visited her in the hospital almost every day and told everyone I could, "Don't worry. Healing is coming." Weeks into her chemo, Lonna asked me if she was doing anything to prevent her healing from happening. She said, "Pastor, I searched my heart to discover any unconfessed sin or unforgiveness toward anyone, and I can't think of anything."

She was such a kind and loving person. It was apparent that she was as sincere as possible. I don't think she had an enemy in the world. As part of our church plant, she attended when less than two dozen people filled our seats. She celebrated our growth as much as anyone and loved the Lord. She loved Hallie more than she loved herself.

I made a deal with her. I said, "Lonna, if you don't give up, I'll do all the praying." So, I did. I prayed and fasted. I would check myself into hotels to cry out to God on her behalf. I rebuked everything I could think to rebuke. I claimed everything I knew to claim. I threw all I had into my intercession.

One day when I went to visit Lonna in the hospital, she was propped up with pillows on her mechanical bed and could hardly find the strength to speak to me. I had to lean down so I could hear her more clearly. Finally, she asked, "Is it okay if I give up now, Pastor Frankie?" My forehead fell onto her bed, and I said, "Yes, Lonna. It's okay."

I stood up and walked down the hall to the small ice machine room, where I put my back against the wall and slid down to the floor. With my hands on my face, I wept. Tears ran down my forearms and made little puddles on the floor.

At Lonna's funeral, my voice repeatedly broke throughout the message I gave. She had told me once that my tears would not roll down if I looked up. I looked up a lot that day, especially when I saw Hallie in the pretty dress her grandma had set aside for her that day. Days before Lonna passed, she had asked me to be Hallie's godfather. It has been a highlight of my life to see Hallie grow up under the shadow of the Highest.

The Lord has paid very careful attention to her. She is an entrepreneur who has built a phenomenal business and holds firm to her faith. I am so proud of her.

To this day, I do not know why Lonna died. I still feel the pain of losing that battle. We were all so desperate to win. I have played what-if scenarios, and I still have more questions than answers nearly a decade later. For a reason only God knows, not everyone who receives prayer gets healed. Sometimes there is indeed something happening that prevents a person from receiving healing. However, placing blame on the person being prayed for is wrong and unfruitful. Placing the blame on God is also wrong. In each case, you are posturing yourself as a judge.

As painful as an unanswered prayer may be, we must remember that our knowledge is limited. This being the case, all we can say is if someone receives healing, it is because of God; if they do not receive healing, all we can do is leave it with God. He is under no obligation to explain Himself to us. I know all the Scriptures that say the sick shall be healed when we pray for them. So far, we just have not seen that reality. Rather than drawing conclusions that are far above our pay grade, let us simply say, "I do not know." That is the safest, most accurate answer we could ever give. We just need enough humility to utter those words.

Kathryn Kuhlman was one of the greatest healing evangelists in American history. The Holy Spirit flowed through and out of her with amazing power into countless people at her crusades. Yet not everyone who came received the healing they

AS PAINFUL AS AN
UNANSWERED PRAYER MAY BE,
WE MUST REMEMBER THAT OUR
KNOWLEDGE IS LIMITED.

had so desperately sought. Joan Gieson, Kulhman's assistant, wrote:

> It goes without saying that many people were healed, but Kathryn didn't want to be praised or recognized for those. Instead, she simply cried out to God, asking why everyone wasn't healed. She didn't allow the healings to boost her ego; rather, her heart broke for those who left without receiving their miracle.[18]

How do we handle the agony of defeat? I have been disappointed, hurt, and upset to tears because the Lord did not answer me the way I wanted, yet I have continued to pray for others' healing. Thousands would still be sick, in pain, and handicapped if I had stopped. What a terrible thought!

We must celebrate everything the Lord does in, through, and among us. The more of His glory we celebrate and the more we pray for the sick, the more we will see. Do you have the fortitude to continue to serve Him amid confusion? I pray that you do. You are of great importance to the Kingdom of God.

---

18. Joan Gieson, *Healing in His Presence: The Untold Secrets of Kathryn Kuhlman's Healing Ministry and Relationship with Holy Spirit* (Shippensburg, PA: Destiny Image Publishers, 2017), 79.

CHAPTER 5: DISCOVERY QUESTIONS

1. In this chapter, we discussed different "elephants in the room," such as speaking in tongues and prophecy. Which topic did you glean from the most?

_____

_____

_____

_____

_____

2. Do you believe these "elephants in the room" have impacted how often we see healings and miracles?

_____

_____

_____

_____

_____

3. As believers, we will experience the thrill of victory (answers to prayers) and the agony of defeat (unanswered prayer). Share an example of each from your personal life.

_____

_____

_____

_____

_____

_____

4. How would you advise a friend to strengthen their faith during difficult seasons?

_____

_____

_____

_____

_____

_____

THORNS, CROSSES, AND GIFTS

Even when general doubts about the supernatural have been assuaged, questions may still linger about whether God intended for you, specifically, to use the spiritual gifts. This chapter will address some of the popular roadblocks that keep people from receiving God's gifts.

First, I am going to answer the statement, "I don't know that the Lord wants to heal me because He didn't remove Paul's thorn." Second, I will respond to those who say, "I believe the trouble I'm facing is simply my cross to bear." Third, I will respond to those who do not believe all Christians are called to move in the gifts of the Spirit.

PAUL'S THORN

Biblical support for the belief that God may not want to heal someone's illness, pain, or handicap, just as He chose not to remove the thorn from Paul, is found in 2 Corinthians:

> *And lest I should be exalted above measure through the abundance of the revelations, there was given to me a thorn in the flesh, the messenger of Satan to buffet me, lest I should be exalted above measure. For this thing I besought the Lord thrice, that it might depart from me. And he said unto me, My grace is sufficient for thee: for my strength is made perfect in weakness. Most gladly therefore will I rather glory in my infirmities, that the power of Christ may rest upon me.*
>
> (2 Corinthians 12:7–9 KJV)

The preceding and subsequent verses show that persecution is the context of the chapter, not sickness. *"A messenger of Satan"* was permitted to buffet Paul, not an illness. The term "buffet" is peppered throughout the New Testament. According to *Strong's Concordance*, the term "buffet" in Greek is translated as *kolaphizó*, which means "to strike with the fist." In the *NAS Exhaustive Concordance*, the definition for "buffet" is "to beat with their fists, harshly treated, roughly treated, torment." Here are some examples of other places in the Bible where the term is used, sharing the same meaning. The emphasis on "buffet" is mine:

+ Matthew 26:67 (KJV): *Then did they spit in his face, and* **buffeted** *him; and others smote him with the palms of their hands.*

+ Mark 14:65 (KJV): *And some began to spit on him, and to cover his face, and to* **buffet** *him, and to say unto him, Prophesy: and the servants did strike him with the palms of their hands.*

+ First Peter 2:20 (KJV): *For what glory is it, if, when ye be* **buffeted** *for your faults, ye shall take it patiently? but if, when ye do well, and suffer for it, ye take it patiently, this is acceptable with God.*

Physical sickness is not implied in any of the above examples. Matthew's and Mark's separate accounts of Jesus's trial before the High Priest Caiaphas shortly before His crucifixion show that the term "buffeting" involves a physical hit. In 1 Peter 2:20, the same term points to a mental strike in the form of guilt and condemnation. Essentially, Paul was "buffeted in the ears," mentally and verbally harassed. Paul prayed three times that the condemning messenger of Satan would depart from him. The messenger might have been a spirit whispering lies or a person possessed with an evil spirit taunting him just as the demon-possessed slave did to Paul and Silas in Acts 16:16–18.

The references to thorns in the Old Testament do not refer to sickness at all, but to human enemies. (See, for example, Numbers 33:55; Joshua 23:13; Judges 2:3.) As Dr. Clark points out in his book *The Healing Breakthrough*, "That makes it even more likely that Paul's thorn in the flesh, which has so often been interpreted as physical sickness or disease, is in fact referring to a person or persons."[19]

The obvious questions are, "Why would God allow the buffeting to take place?" and "Why not command the messenger to flee?" Paul answered these questions for us:

And lest I should be exalted above measure through the abundance of the revelations, there was given to me a thorn in the flesh, the messenger of Satan to buffet me, lest I should be exalted above measure.   (2 Corinthians 12:7 KJV)

In other words, Paul received such a great revelation that a messenger was sent to harass him to keep him humble.

Keep in mind the amazing things Paul witnessed in his walk with God. First, his conversion began by hearing the voice of Jesus Christ. (See Acts 9:5.) Second, Paul received his call to preach directly from Jesus. (See Galatians 1:12.) Third, he was permitted to visit the third heaven. (See 2 Corinthians 12:1–4.) Such privileges could make the godliest among us proud. Therefore, the Lord allowed the messenger from Satan to keep Paul humble.

When I hear someone say their sickness has been allowed, just like Paul's thorn was allowed to remain, I ask, "Have you also received similar revelations so grand that you're tempted to

19. Randy Clark, *The Healing Breakthrough* (Bloomington, MN: Chosen Books, 2016), 34.

THE REFERENCES TO THORNS
IN THE OLD TESTAMENT DO NOT
REFER TO SICKNESS AT ALL,
BUT TO HUMAN ENEMIES.

be arrogant?" Unless you have received Paul's blessing, do not assume that you have received his burden.

MY CROSS TO BEAR

I am sure that you have heard people say, "Everyone has a cross that they must bear." This is usually said in reference to sickness, disease, financial challenges, strained relationships within families or among close friends, or something else that is consistently difficult. In most cases, they are referring to these words of Jesus:

> *If anyone comes to Me and does not hate his father and mother, wife and children, brothers and sisters, yes, and his own life also, he cannot be My disciple. And whoever does not bear his cross and come after Me cannot be My disciple. For which of you, intending to build a tower, does not sit down first and count the cost, whether he has enough to finish it.* (Luke 14:26–28 NKJV)

Jesus was speaking to the crowds following Him about the importance of knowing the cost before choosing to become one of His disciples. The message was wrapped around sacrificing personal desires entirely to submit to the will of God.

There is no thought of sickness, illness, or hardship in the passage. The cross Jesus is talking about is something that you take up as a choice in following Him. You do not have to take up a hardship or sickness to follow Him. If that had been a requirement, then the cross would not do all that the Lord promised us. As foretold by the prophet Isaiah:

He was wounded for our transgressions, He was bruised for our iniquities; the chastisement for our peace was upon Him, and by His stripes we are healed.

(Isaiah 53:5 NKJV)

If you have not received the manifestation of your healing or deliverance from trouble, I implore you not to build a false theology that makes you feel more comfortable with your unanswered prayer. Instead, choose to say, "I don't know why my prayer hasn't been answered yet. I know this illness, this oppression, is not God's will. Therefore, with my last breath, I will continue to pray, worship, and listen to the Holy Spirit to know if I should do anything further." Then, the day you experience the fullness of God's love toward you, you will know that He would never want you to live one second in agony.

In the meantime, choose to live by faith. Your faith, as small as it may be, has power. (See Matthew 17:20.)

GIFTS, OFFICES, AND ACCESS

The last roadblock we will cover sounds the most spiritual. It relates to whether God wants to give spiritual gifts such as prophecy, healing, miracles, speaking in tongues, a word of wisdom, and so on. It is easy to believe that if God wanted you to have a spiritual gift, you would have it already, that you should not need to pray for it. However, God *does* want you to use spiritual gifts. It is part of His conditional will for you.

The things of God are gained through pursuit in prayer and meditation on His Word. Jesus said, *"If you abide in me, and my words abide in you, ask whatever you wish, and it will be done for you"* (John 15:7 ESV). God does want you to have spiritual gifts, but He also *wants you to want them,* which is evident in His desire for you to let His words *"abide in you."*

This does not mean that you will receive every spiritual gift in equal measure through prayer. Some are given more spiritual authority than others to fulfill specific callings. The supporting reference is found in 1 Corinthians 12:29–31:

> *Are we all apostles? Are we all prophets? Are we all teachers? Do we all have the power to do miracles? Do we all have the gift of healing? Do we all have the ability to speak in unknown languages? Do we all have the ability to interpret unknown languages? Of course not! So you should earnestly desire the most helpful gifts.*

Spiritual gifts are given to saints through an impartation for the work of the ministry. (See Romans 12:6; 1 Corinthians 12:8–10.) These differ from people who are assigned to *be* gifts to the church within one of the five offices: apostle, prophet, evangelist, pastor, and teacher. (See Ephesians 4:7–12.) Those who are in these offices are responsible for training and equipping the church at large to grow both in maturity and within the gifts of the Spirit so we can all bear fruit as true disciples and bring great glory to the Father. (See John 15:8.)

GOD DOES WANT YOU TO HAVE
SPIRITUAL GIFTS,
BUT HE ALSO WANTS YOU
TO WANT THEM, TO LET HIS
WORDS "ABIDE IN YOU."

You cannot and should not choose to be in one of the five offices unless you know that you were born for such a purpose and have been ordained or chosen based on specific qualifications. (See Acts 6:3; 14:23; 1 Timothy 3; Titus 1:5–9.) I have been asked how I knew that I was called to be a pastor. My response is, "Pastoring isn't something you necessarily want to do. It's something you know you *must* do."

Spiritual gifts, on the other hand, are available for all believers. Your desires will help you identify which of the gifts you are supposed to have. For example, I have a great desire to see people receive physical healing. I have a close friend who does not share my passion; rather, he is drawn to the prophetic.

A need that breaks your heart is an indication of the gift the Lord desires to give you. You may also notice, as I did, that as seasons change in your life, so will your desire for particular gifts. Early on in our ministry, I was primarily focused on pastoring a local church. Over the last ten years, I have found a great love for missions, particularly in South America.

The people you want to reach for Jesus are also an indication of which spiritual gift you need. I have a friend who gets paid a lot of money to sit down with CEOs of Fortune 500 companies and give them counsel concerning their billion-dollar organizations. Out of sheer necessity, an assignment like that would require the gifts of discerning of spirits, words of wisdom, and words of knowledge. (See 1 Corinthians 12:8–10.)

Even though you may gravitate toward certain gifts, some are available to you regardless of your desires. Some gifts are for all of us. Wisdom is promised to those who ask. (See James 1:5.) Likewise, the gift of healing should be one of the signs that follow you as a believer. (See Mark 16:17–18.)

You may notice that some people have been given a great anointing for one of the gifts so that they may produce more fruit in that area than you. For example, take Billy Graham's ministry compared to my own. Before his passing, Graham held crusades in baseball stadiums and had more conversions in one day than I will have in years. Clearly, he had a great anointing to be an evangelist and save the lost. I do not have that same anointing. However, that does not mean that I should not share the gospel with my family and friends.

Regardless of how evangelistically anointed we may be, we should all accept the Great Commission:

> Therefore, go and make disciples of all the nations, baptizing them in the name of the Father and the Son and the Holy Spirit. Teach these new disciples to obey all the commands I have given you.　　　　(Matthew 28:19–20)

There may be people who have a greater anointing within a spiritual gift than you do. However, that does not mean that you do not need the same gift.

SPIRITUAL GIFTS ARE FOR YOU

If you need further confirmation that spiritual gifts are for you, let us review what we already know:

+ You are called to be a light to the lost in this dark world. (See Matthew 5:14.)

+ You are called to make disciples. (See Matthew 28:19–20.)

+ God anointed Jesus with the Holy Spirit and with power, the disciples received power, and Paul ministered in power. (See, respectively, Acts 10:38; 14:3; 1 Corinthians 2:4.)

It is no wonder that Paul prayed that we too would have *"the power to accomplish all the good things"* our faith compels us to do (2 Thessalonians 1:11).

It is easy to live for the Lord without pursuing any spiritual gifts. In many ways, it is more challenging to go for the spiritual gifts and dig deep to discover the secrets and mature things hidden in the Word. The road less traveled is the road into the unseen world. I want to challenge you by saying, go for it! Do not turn your back on the gifts of the Spirit.

Partnering with Jesus in the supernatural will lead to some of the most exhilarating moments in your life. Looking into the teary eyes of someone who was blessed, healed, or delivered the moment you prayed for them will fill you with immeasurable joy. God *"has invited you into partnership with his Son, Jesus Christ our Lord"* (1 Corinthians 1:9). This invitation is the greatest of all opportunities. You were not born to make money, build a house, laugh, and die. You have a supernatural assignment—and as I've said before, you will need supernatural gifts to complete that assignment.

CHAPTER 6: DISCOVERY QUESTIONS

1. Now that you know more about Paul's thorn, how would you explain it to others?

_____

_____

_____

_____

_____

2. How would you respond if you heard someone refer to their sickness or difficulty as "their cross to bear"?

_____

_____

_____

_____

_____

3. How would you explain to others that spiritual gifts are for all believers?

_____

_____

_____

_____

_____

_____

4. What spiritual gift or gifts do you desire most? How would you use this gift or gifts?

_____

_____

_____

_____

_____

7

NORMAL CHRISTIANITY

Everyone has a unique, God-given assignment. Every Christian also shares the call to make disciples. Even when we may think that the world is too far gone, Christian hope must prevail. God's love and power are enough to turn hearts we have given up on.

God has continuously used faithful remnants to change nations. The faithful remnant has always been identified by their passion and their conviction, resonating with the prophet Jeremiah:

> *But if I say I'll never mention the* Lord *or speak in his name, his word burns in my heart like a fire. It's like a fire in my bones! I am worn out trying to hold it in! I can't do it!*
> (Jeremiah 20:9)

A faithful remnant will stir up the revival that the church has been praying for—just like the revival that set me on the path I follow now. The Brownsville Revival started in a Sunday morning church service. The only thing special about that day, June 18, 1995, was that it happened to be Father's Day. Still, God chose that day to move. A small group of Brownsville Church attendees, led by Pastor John Kilpatrick, had met faithfully on Sunday nights for two years, praying for the revival that broke out in that Father's Day service. Night after night, for years, the Spirit of the Lord met people powerfully at Brownsville Church. People encountered God in ways they never had before. It was the longest-running revival in the history of America. Media outlets began to report on what was unexplainable with earthly knowledge. Pastors from around the country heard of what God was doing and began to believe for it in their churches.

My pastors, Randy and Reneé Clark, began to believe for revival in our church. They prayed that God would move powerfully in our city. And He did. In 1996, revival broke out in Triumph Church in Nederland, Texas. I was a senior in high school then. It was my last semester, and I spent most of my time outside of school with my best friends, Jason and Matthew. We all grew up believing Jesus was our Lord and Savior, but you

THE HOLY SPIRIT STARTED
MOVING SOVEREIGNLY AT
TRIUMPH CHURCH.
WE WERE OVERWHELMED AND
IN CONSTANT AWE OF HIS
PRESENCE.

would not have known that had you seen us on weekends. If it was wrong, we were doing it. If it was right, we were not doing it. I was half-drowned in a whirlpool of abominable sins until God met me in a revival service.

The Holy Spirit started moving sovereignly at Triumph Church night after night for a month. For three to six hours each night, we were overwhelmed and in constant awe of His presence. If I were to speak of what His presence was like every day for the rest of my life, I still could not adequately describe how exhilarating and powerful those services were. Planned sermons went by the wayside. The worship team sang only sporadically. We all knew the Holy Spirit was leading the service. Most often, the congregation was simply sitting, standing, or kneeling, arrested by the manifestation of His love.

At the same time, the Spirit of the Lord was performing surgery on my heart. In a moment, all that I am—my mind, my heart, my will, and my desires—were transformed into a new person. Two weeks before the end of my senior year, I was sitting in an English class—in the front row, where the teacher made me sit because I was *that* kid—when I turned to Matthew, who was sitting in the seat behind me. I said, "Matthew, the day after we graduate, you'll never see me again."

He laughed because he thought I was joking. He started going on about how we needed to stick together and never lose touch. But I had meant what I said. When Matthew realized that I was not laughing with him, he asked me why I told him that. I replied, "I don't know, but you'll never see me again. I'll promise you that."

I never did see him again. I lost touch with Jason too after that. God's power did not simply create a spiritual high that I would become nostalgic about later. His power created a lasting impact on my life. The faithful remnant who ignited the revival in Brownsville spread to Triumph Church in Nederland and radically changed my life forever.

That is the power of a remnant devoted to God. The faithful remnant does not stop hearing from God or believing in His vision simply because of the worries of the world or the lure of wealth. Their hearts are not like the thorny ground mentioned in the parable of the sower. (See Matthew 13:22.) The remnant does not need to return to God or be brought back to life in a revival. Their vigorous faith has kept their footing firm. Instead, such outpourings introduce them to deeper levels of intimacy and most often empower them for effective ministry.

A faithful remnant is like the center of a radar scanner display. They continuously sense the presence of God and are faithful to His laws. (See Matthew 22:36–40.) God's presence does not simply stay with them, but it expands outward in concentric circles, affecting the geography around them. When God wants to move in a big way, He starts with a faithful remnant—no matter the size.

In the Bible, God used Noah's family to establish a new covenant. (See Genesis 9.) He used Ezra, Nehemiah, and those with them to rebuild the land promised to the Israelites. (See the books of Ezra and Nehemiah.) Simeon and Anna represented a faithful remnant of those who had not been so overcome by the legality of the Law as to deny their Savior. (See Luke 2:25–38.)

Every revival in modern times began with a faithful remnant set apart.

There is a faithful remnant now, just as there has been in every generation since Christ's resurrection. This faithful remnant, as Paul wrote, is *"a remnant chosen by grace"* (Romans 11:5 NIV). We, God's people, have all been chosen by grace. We can each be a part of the faithful remnant if we desire to be. God desires to move through us in love and in power to reach all of His children, even those who have not chosen Him. The next revival, outpouring, or Great Awakening will come through us. Earmarks of the remnant of our age will be:

+ We will protect our daily appointment to be alone with God and stay in communion with the Holy Spirit throughout our day, as we *"pray in the Spirit at all times and on every occasion"* (Ephesians 6:18).

+ We refuse to be amused by, or associate with, anything Jesus died to overcome. *"Because we belong to the day, we must live decent lives for all to see"* (Romans 13:13).

+ Our passion for God will be like lightning in our veins and *"fire in* [our] *bones"* (Jeremiah 20:9).

+ We will no longer depend on our natural strengths and abilities because *"the LORD will be* [our] *confidence"* (Proverbs 3:26 NKJV).

+ We will devote every part of our body to be used *"as an instrument to do what is right for the glory of God"* (Romans 6:13).

GOD DESIRES TO MOVE
THROUGH US IN LOVE AND IN
POWER TO REACH ALL OF HIS
CHILDREN, EVEN THOSE
WHO HAVE NOT CHOSEN HIM.

◆ Lastly, we will never forget that we have been chosen to be *"the light of the world"* (Matthew 5:14). We refuse to live hidden. We will be courageous and daring as we share our faith with others.

I could not have dreamed the life God had in store for me when I said goodbye to my old life. I walked away from my closest friends. I walked away not moving toward anything or anyone other than God. I walked alone for a while before I found other believers walking in the same direction. And it was worth it.

Ultimately, when we hunger for more of God in our lives—more of His love and more of His power—it should be a prayer for us to be used as clay vessels for Him to move through in love at will. (See 2 Corinthians 4:7.) This is the way that we can live as Jesus did. Power moved through Him not simply to awe and amaze but to save us, *"doing good and healing all who were oppressed by the devil"* (Acts 10:38). The disciples moved in power to build God's church.

When you pray to see God's supernatural power in your life, *"this hope will not lead to disappointment"* (Romans 5:5). *"For God is working in you, giving you the desire and the power to do what pleases him"* (Philippians 2:13).

When I left my friendships with Jason and Matthew, I really left them...but God did not leave them. After twenty-six years of no contact with Jason, he found me on social media. He saw that I was a pastor and just could not believe what his eyes saw, so he messaged me, trying to figure out how it could be that a Frankie Mazzapica was leading Celebration Church.

He determined that I was *the* Frankie who he knew—the one with whom he graduated from Nederland High School. He still did not quite believe it, so he brought his fiancée with him on a ninety-minute drive to see me preach. At the time, he had been a attending a nondenominational church for about three months. I had not even known whether he still practiced any religion.

During the service, I was too nervous to look in Jason's direction. Seeing him in the crowd threw me off that much. When I got to the end of my message, I opened the altar and began a time of ministry, still focusing on not making eye contact with Jason or his fiancée. However, I did see him when I turned around to look at the other side of the altar. I saw streams of tears coming down his face as he worshipped with his hands raised. His fiancée was in tears too. That is what the power of God does.

Later, they texted to tell me how much the service had impacted them—but it was not my sermon that affected them. Instead, the presence of God moved in an undeniable way. One verse comes to mind:

> *My message and my preaching were not with wise and persuasive words, but with a demonstration of the Spirit's power.* (1 Corinthians 2:4 NIV)

God takes our natural and gives it a supernatural impact. Without God's power moving through me that Sunday, I could have given the most theologically correct, most engaging sermon ever, with lots of stories and jokes, and still not have moved a single heart. On our own, our gifts and talents are not enough. But with God, we can do more than is conceivable. (See Ephesians 3:20.)

Most of you reading this book probably have someone in your life whose salvation you have been praying for. I have a few of those people. Even if you do not have someone you are praying for, you have probably come into contact with people who seem so far gone that you know God Himself would have to soften their hearts for them to come to Christ.

Those of us who have regular conversations with non-Christians know that their decision to not attend church on Sunday is not consciously made. They do not say, "No, I won't go to church today" because the question of going to church never crosses their mind. As they drive down the road, they do not notice the churches they pass. Therefore, our presence in their lives is the closest they may ever get to experiencing the Spirit of the Lord.

When the church comes together, in the sanctuary or in small groups, we must expect that God will move among us. All believers should have testimonies of God demonstrating His power through their prayers. Let it be that unbelievers will walk through a church's doors and *"fall to their knees and worship God, declaring, 'God is truly here among you'"* (1 Corinthians 14:25). That is what a "normal" church should look like.

A predictable, cookie-cutter church service—one with a set number of rehearsed songs, a few announcements, an offering, and a concise sermon—should not be a part of our culture. We all know that God wants more from us individually as well as corporately. Though our lives and our services may always have

ON OUR OWN, OUR GIFTS AND
TALENTS ARE NOT ENOUGH.
BUT WITH GOD,
WE CAN DO MORE
THAN IS CONCEIVABLE.

certain necessary components, may the impromptu nudge of the Holy Spirit disrupt our preplanned agenda and be a regular occurrence.

The Spirit of the Lord outlined what normal Christianity should look like in the Scriptures. (See Acts 2:46; Matthew 28:19–20.) The New Testament church regularly demonstrated God's love and power. (See Luke 10:9; John 14:12; Mark 9:23; 16:17–18.)

Wherever we are is where we should expect to see God move. William Booth is credited with saying, "I am not waiting for a move of God; I am a move of God." We are the move of God. *You* are the move of God. I pray that you live that way.

CHAPTER 7: DISCOVERY QUESTIONS

1. What type of Christians does Satan fear?

_____

_____

_____

_____

_____

2. Jerimiah said that God's word burned in his heart like fire in his bones. (See Jeremiah 20:9.) How do you think those words fleshed out in his life?

_____

_____

_____

_____

_____

3. What adjustments do you need to make in your life to cultivate a burning passion for the presence of God?

_____

_____

_____

_____

_____

_____

4. How do you believe the Lord desires to partner with you?

_____

_____

_____

_____

_____

_____

ABOUT THE AUTHOR

Houston native Frankie Mazzapica is the founding and lead pastor of Celebration Church of The Woodlands, Texas. Three people from the community were in attendance on the day that Frankie and his wife Allie launched the church in 2005.

Today, Celebration Church is a vibrant, multiplying community of believers. People experience a demonstration of God's power in the form of physical healings, changed lives, emotional restoration, and deliverance. Celebration's momentum and footprint continue to expand rapidly with multiple in-person services and a vast array of attention-grabbing digital platforms. Frankie's encouraging, challenging, and humorous messages are nationally broadcast each Sunday on TBN.

Frankie has more than twenty-five years of experience in full-time ministry. Prior to planting their church, he and Allie served on pastoral staff with Joel and Victoria Osteen at Lakewood Church.

Frankie's conviction is that Jesus's three-year ministry, where teaching and miracles attracted seekers and built disciples, is the model for today's church. Believers should not rest until the same power displayed in the life of the Lord's disciples is present in their lives. Frankie's mission statement is, "I live to walk with the Lord and share His love and His power."

Your Divine Invitation: Access the Holy Spirit to Complete Your Assignment is Frankie's first book. He wanted to share the practical steps every believer can take to position themselves to receive God's promised endowment of power.

Frankie and Allie were married in 2001. They have two girls and one boy: Preslee, Luke, and Kate. They love the blend of urban and suburban life in The Woodlands, but they've built their home a half-hour away in the country, where one can see the shooting stars in the Texas night sky.

TO CONNECT WITH FRANKIE, VISIT:

 **FACEBOOK**

@PrFrankieMazzapica

INSTAGRAM

frankie.mazzapica

YOUTUBE

FrankieMazzapicaNOW

TIKTOK

frankiemazzapica

WHAT THE AUTHOR SAYS ABOUT POWER FROM GOD...

Power from God by Charles Finney is the book that changed my life forever and provoked me to pursue and activate gifts of the Spirit in my life. Before becoming the leading evangelist of the nineteenth century, he was one of the few chosen by God to spark the Second Great Awakening. Finney later wrote of the moment he received an impartation of power:

> The Holy Spirit descended upon me in as manner that seemed to go through me, body and soul. I could feel the impression, like a wave of electricity, going through me. Indeed, it seemed to come in waves of liquid love—I cannot express it in any other way. It seemed like the very breath of God.

Finney boldly speaks of how Christians, even church leaders, have learned to live without receiving a divine impartation of power. Consequently, they can only partially fulfill God's full assignment for their lives.

If you long to walk closer with the Lord and see the manifestation of His presence when you pray, I challenge you to read *Power from God*. You will clearly understand the conditions that must be met before receiving all the Holy Spirit desires to give you. I believe it will change your life as it has countless others, including mine.

—*Frankie Mazzapica*

The

COMPLETE
LAUGH
-OUT-
LOUD
JOKES
for
KIDS

The COMPLETE LAUGH -OUT- LOUD JOKES for KIDS

* A 4-in-1 Collection *

ROB ELLIOTT

Revell
a division of Baker Publishing Group
Grand Rapids, Michigan

© 2010, 2012, 2013, 2014 by Robert E. Teigen

Published by Revell
a division of Baker Publishing Group
P.O. Box 6287, Grand Rapids, MI 49516-6287
www.revellbooks.com

ISBN 978-0-8007-6988-8

Previously published in four separate volumes:
Laugh-Out-Loud Jokes for Kids (2010) by Rob Elliott
Zoolarious Animal Jokes for Kids (2012) by Rob Elliott
Knock-Knock Jokes for Kids (2013) by Rob Elliott
More Laugh-Out-Loud Jokes for Kids (2014) by Rob Elliott

Printed in the United States of America

The poem "Ode to a Cricket" is used by permission.

14   15   16   17   18   19   20   7   6   5   4   3   2

CONTENTS

1

LAUGH -OUT- LOUD JOKES *for* KIDS

Q & A Jokes

Q: **Why did the robber wash his clothes before he ran away with the loot?**

A: He wanted to make a clean getaway.

Q: **How does a skeleton call his friends?**

A: On the tele-bone.

Q: **What is the richest kind of air?**

A: A millionaire.

Q: **Who keeps the ocean clean?**

A: The mermaid.

Q: **Why did the invisible man turn down a job offer?**

A: He just couldn't see himself doing it.

Q: Why did the skeleton drink eight glasses of milk every day?

A: Milk is good for the bones.

Q: Why did Johnny jump up and down before he drank his juice?

A: The carton said to "shake well before drinking."

Q: What is a baby's favorite reptile?

A: A rattlesnake.

Q: What does a snowman eat for breakfast?

A: Frosted Flakes.

Q: Where do generals keep their armies?

A: In their sleevies.

Q: How do you make a hot dog stand?

A: Take away its chair.

Q: What kind of balls don't bounce?

A: Eyeballs.

Q: Why can't you play hide-and-seek with mountains?

A: Because they're always peaking.

Q: What did the bride say when she dropped her bouquet?

A: "Whoopsy-Daisies."

Q: Why did Jimmy's parents scream when they saw his grades?

A: Because he had a bee on his report card.

Q: What do you call a stick that won't do anything you want?

A: A stick-in-the-mud.

Q: What do you get when you cross a pig and a centipede?

A: Bacon and legs.

Q: What do you get when you cross a tiger and a snowman?

A: Frostbite!

Q: What is a duck on the Fourth of July?

A: A fire-quacker.

Q: Why did the credit card go to jail?

A: It was guilty as charged.

Q: What would we get if we threw all the books in the ocean?

A: A title wave!

Q: What do you call a liar on the phone?

A: A telephony.

Q: What do peanut butter and jelly do around the campfire?

A: They tell toast stories.

Q: What did the baker say when he found the dough he'd lost?

A: "That's just what I kneaded!"

Q: Why did the flashlight, the camera, and the remote-controlled car attend the funeral?

A: They were grieving the dead batteries.

Q: Why wouldn't the team play with the third basketball?

A: Because it was an odd ball.

Q: Where do electric bills like to go on vacation?

A: I-Owe-A (Iowa).

Q: Why did the queen go to the dentist?

A: To get crowns on her teeth.

Q: How did the lobster get to the ocean?

A: By shell-icopter.

Q: When does the road get angry?

A: When someone crosses it.

Q: Why was the king only a foot tall?

A: Because he was a ruler.

Q: What did the robber say when he stole from the bookstore?

A: "I had better book it out of here."

Q: Why did Sally's computer keep sneezing?

A: It had a virus.

Q: When do doctors get mad?

A: When they lose their patients (patience).

Q: Why did Jimmy throw the clock out the window?

A: He wanted to see time fly.

Q: What language does a billboard speak?

A: Sign language.

Q: Why didn't the girl trust the ocean?

A: There was something fishy about it.

Q: What do you call four bullfighters in quicksand?

A: Cuatro sinko.

Q: How did the baseball player lose his house?

A: He made his home run.

Q: Who was the only person in the Bible without a father?

A: Joshua, because he was the son of Nun (none).

Q: Why did the man put his money in the freezer?

A: He wanted some cold hard cash.

Q: What did the one-dollar bill say to the ten-dollar bill?

A: You don't make any cents (sense).

Q: What happens when race car drivers eat too much?

A: They get Indy-gestion.

Q: Why do baseball pitchers stay away from caves?
A: They don't like bats.

Q: What kind of tree has the best bark?
A: A dogwood.

Q: What kind of makeup do pirate girls wear?
A: Ship gloss.

Q: When do you need Chapstick in the garden?
A: When you're planting the tulips (two lips).

Q: Why did the trees take a nap?
A: For rest (forest).

Q: What is a zucchini's favorite game?
A: Squash.

Q: Why wouldn't the lion eat the clown?
A: He tasted funny.

Q: What kinds of hats do you wear on your legs?
A: Knee caps.

Q: How do you reach a book in an emergency?

A: Call its pager.

Q: Who helped the monster go to the ball?

A: Its scary godmother.

Q: Why did the banana wear sunscreen at the beach?

A: It didn't want to peel.

Q: Where does a ship go when it's not feeling well?

A: To see the dock-tor.

Q: Why was the nose feeling sad?

A: It was tired of getting picked on.

Q: What did the elevator say to its friend?

A: "I think I'm coming down with something."

Q: Why did Billy have a hot dog in his shoe?

A: It was a foot-long.

Q: What gets wet while it dries?

A: A towel.

Q: How did the farmer fix his jeans?

A: With a cabbage patch.

Q: What do you call a silly doorbell?

A: A ding-dong.

Q: What did the sock say to the foot?

A: "Shoe!"

Q: When do you stop at green and go on red?

A: When you're eating a watermelon.

Q: What did one tube of glue say to the other?

A: "Let's stick together."

Q: What did one wall say to the other?

A: "Let's meet at the corner!"

Q: Did you hear about the red ship and blue ship that collided?

A: All the sailors were marooned.

Q: Why did the girl need a ladder to go to school?

A: Because it was high school.

Q: What do sea monsters eat?

A: Fish and ships.

Q: What does a computer do when it's tired?

A: It crashes.

Q: What did the tooth fairy use to fix her wand?

A: Toothpaste.

Q: Why did the computer get glasses?

A: To improve his web sight.

Q: What stays in the corner but travels all over the world?

A: A stamp.

Q: What did the computer say when it fell into quicksand?

A: "Help me! I'm syncing!"

Q: What do you get when you have two doctors at once?

A: Pair-a-medics.

Q: What should you do when you get in a jam?

A: Grab some bread and peanut butter.

Q: How can you go surfing in the kitchen?

A: On a micro-wave.

Q: Why was everyone looking up at the ceiling and cheering?

A: They were ceiling fans.

Q: Why did the cowboy go out and buy a wiener dog?

A: Because someone told him to "get a *long*, little doggie."

Q: What is a trombone's favorite playground equipment?

A: The slide.

Q: How can you keep someone in suspense?

A: I'll tell you later.

Q: What happened to the beans when they showed up late to work?

A: They got canned.

Q: Why can't you take anything balloons say seriously?

A: They're always full of hot air.

Q: What happens when you phone a clown three times?

A: You get a three-ring circus.

Q: What do you get when you have breakfast with a centipede?

A: Pancakes and legs.

Q: What do you call someone who is afraid of picnics?

A: A basket case.

Q: How does an Eskimo fix his broken toys?

A: With igloo.

Q: What kind of flowers are great friends?

A: Rose buds.

Q: What do you get when you cross a tuba, a drum, and a spare tire?

A: A rubber band.

Q: Why did the lady sing lullabies to her purse?

A: She wanted a sleeping bag.

Q: What did the orange say to the banana when they were looking for the apple?

A: Keep your eyes peeled.

Q: Did you hear about the teacher who was cross-eyed?

A: She couldn't control her pupils.

Q: What kinds of teeth cost money?

A: Buck teeth.

Q: What do you call a dentist who cleans an alligator's teeth?

A: Crazy!

Q: If a snake married an undertaker, what would they embroider on their towels?

A: Hiss and Hearse (his and hers).

Q: What is the difference between boogers and broccoli?

A: Kids won't eat their broccoli.

Q: What do elves learn in kindergarten?

A: The elf-abet.

Q: Why did the golfer wear two pairs of pants?

A: In case he got a hole in one.

Q: Why didn't the skeleton go to the ball?

A: He had no body to dance with.

Q: What kind of beans don't grow in a garden?

A: Jelly beans.

Q: Why can't a nose be twelve inches long?

A: If it was, then it would be a foot.

Q: When does your dinner never get hot?

A: When it's chili.

Q: Why did the boys shoot their BB guns in the air?

A: They wanted to shoot the breeze.

Q: Why were the Cheerios scared of the man?

A: He was a cereal killer.

Q: Why did the baseball player go to jail?

A: He stole second base.

Q: Why couldn't the twelve-year-old go to the pirate movie?

A: It was rated arrrgh.

Q: How did Benjamin Franklin feel about discovering electricity?

A: He was shocked.

Q: What do you call cheese that doesn't belong to you?

A: Nacho cheese.

Q: How much did the butcher charge for his venison?

A: A buck.

Q: What does a rain cloud wear under its clothes?

A: Thunderwear.

Q: How did Thomas Edison invent the lightbulb?

A: He got a bright idea.

Q: Why did the lettuce win the race?

A: He was a head.

Q: Where did the most talkative people in the Bible live?

A: Babylon (babble on).

Q: Why was the broom late for school?

A: It over-swept.

Q: What did the alien say to the flower bed?

A: "Take me to your weeder."

Q: What kind of button won't you find at a sewing store?

A: A belly button.

Q: Why did the lady throw her butter out the window?

A: She wanted to see a butterfly.

Q: Why did the ninja go to the doctor?

A: He had kung-flu.

Q: What did the grape do when the lemon asked for a kiss?

A: It puckered up.

Q: Why couldn't the monster go to sleep?

A: It was afraid there were kids under the bed.

Q: How long does it take to count four times infinity?

A: Four-ever.

Q: Who fills your tank at the gas station?

A: Philip (fill up).

Q: What is an alien's favorite kind of candy?

A: A Mars bar.

Q: How do you get a skeleton to laugh out loud?

A: Tickle its funny bone.

Q: What do you take before every meal?

A: You take a seat.

Q: What did the mother corn say to her children?

A: "Don't forget to wash behind your ears."

Q: Did you hear about the actor who fell through the floor?

A: It was just a stage he was going through.

Q: What did the tomato say to the mushroom?

A: "You look like a fungi."

Q: Why are babies so good at basketball?

A: Because they like to dribble.

Teacher: Name two days of the week that start with a "t."

Student: Today and tomorrow.

Teacher: Billy, you missed school yesterday.

Billy: Well, to tell you the truth, I didn't miss it that much at all.

Fred: Today the teacher was yelling at me for something I didn't do.

Mike: What was that?

Fred: My homework.

Q: Why did the cookie complain about feeling sick?

A: He was feeling crummy.

Q: Why is spaghetti the smartest food there is?

A: It always uses its noodle.

Q: What do you call a student who never turns in his math homework on time?

A: A calcu-later.

Q: How did the karate teacher greet his students?

A: "Hi-Yah!"

Q: Why did the bed wear a disguise?

A: It was undercover.

Q: What do you call a boomerang that doesn't come back?

A: A stick.

Q: **When do pine trees like to do embroidery?**
A: When they do needlepoint.

Q: **What is a baby's motto?**
A: If at first you don't succeed, cry, cry again.

Q: **Where do you keep your jokes?**
A: In a giggle box.

Q: **Why did the lady wear a helmet every time she ate?**
A: She was on a crash diet.

Q: **Why did the hot dog turn down the chance to star in a movie?**
A: None of the roles (rolls) were good enough.

Josh: **Did you hear about the restaurant on the moon?**
Anna: What about it?
Josh: **It has great food but no atmosphere.**

Q: **What do you call a fairy that doesn't take a bath?**
A: Stinkerbell.

Q: **What did one candle say to the other?**
A: "Do you want to go out tonight?"

Q: What is a plumber's favorite vegetable?

A: A leek.

Q: How did the French fry propose to the hamburger?

A: He gave her an onion ring.

Q: What has four legs and one head but only one foot?

A: A bed.

Q: What do potatoes wear to bed?

A: Yammies.

Q: What fruit teases people a lot?

A: A bana na na na na na!

Q: Why was the metal wire so upset?

A: It was getting all bent out of shape over nothing.

Q: What do you call the story of the three little pigs?

A: A pigtail.

Q: What did the peanut butter say to the bread?

A: "Quit loafing around."

Q: What did the bread say back to the peanut butter?

A: "I think you're nuts."

Q: What kind of lights did Noah use on the ark?

A: Flood lights.

Q: How did the orange get into the crowded restaurant?

A: He squeezed his way in.

Q: Why can't the bank keep a secret?

A: It has too many tellers.

Q: Why was the sewing machine so funny?

A: It kept everyone in stitches.

Q: Why did the hamburger always lose the race?

A: It could never ketchup.

Q: How do you punish a naughty eyeball?

A: Give it fifty lashes.

Q: Why was the rope so stressed out?

A: It was getting itself all tied in knots.

Q: What did the math book say to the psychiatrist?

A: "Would you like to hear my problems?"

Q: What do you call a fossil that never does any work?

A: A lazy bones.

Q: What did the pen say to the pencil?

A: "You're sure looking sharp today."

Q: What is green and can sing?

A: Elvis Parsley.

Q: Why didn't the string ever win a race?

A: It was always tied.

Q: What is the best food to eat when you're scared?

A: I scream.

Q: How do you get a tissue to dance?

A: Put a little boogie in it.

Q: What did the tree say to the flower?

A: "I'm rooting for you."

Q: **What is the craziest way to travel?**

A: By loco-motive.

Q: **What did the paper say to the pencil?**

A: "You've got a good point."

Q: **What is the cheapest way to travel?**

A: By sale-boat.

Q: **Who are the cleanest people in the choir?**

A: The soap-ranos.

Q: **What is the noisiest game you can play?**

A: Racket-ball.

Q: **What did the earthquake say to the tornado?**

A: "Don't look at me, it's not my fault."

Q: **What did the tree say to the lumberjack?**

A: "Leaf me alone!"

Q: **Why was it so hot in the stadium after the baseball game?**

A: All the fans left.

Q: Why did the ice cream cone become a reporter?

A: He wanted to get the scoop.

Q: What did the ice cream cone ride to the store?

A: A fudge-cycle.

Q: What kind of poles can swim?

A: Tadpoles.

Q: Why wouldn't the teddy bear eat anything?

A: He was already stuffed.

Q: How does a gingerbread man make his bed?

A: With a cookie sheet.

Q: What do you get when you cross an elephant with Darth Vader?

A: An ele-Vader.

Q: What do cowboys like on their salad?

A: Ranch dressing.

Q: Why was the elf crying?

A: He stubbed his mistle-toe.

Q: How do you make an orange giggle?

A: Tickle its navel.

Q: What kind of candy is never on time?

A: Choco-late.

Q: What kind of music does a boulder like?

A: Rock-n-roll.

Q: What did the mommy rope say to the baby rope?

A: "Don't be knotty."

Q: What do you call a monster with a high IQ?

A: Frank-Einstein.

Q: What did the turkey say to the ham?

A: "Nice to meat you!"

Q: Why was the Incredible Hulk so good at gardening?

A: He had a green thumb.

Q: What did the pool say to the lake?

A: "Water you doing here?"

Q: What did the cake say to the knife?

A: "Do you want a piece of me?"

Q: What was the math teacher's favorite dessert?

A: Pi.

Q: What does bread wear to bed?

A: Jam-mies.

Q: Who earns a living driving their customers away?

A: Taxi drivers.

Q: What did the lumberjack say to the tree?

A: "I have an axe to grind with you."

Customer: Excuse me, waiter, but is there spaghetti on the menu?

Waiter: No, but I believe we have some in the kitchen.

Q: What was the best time of day in the Middle Ages?

A: Knight-time.

Q: What is the fastest peanut butter in the world?

A: Jiffy.

Q: Why was the baseball player a bad sport?

A: He stole third base and then went home.

Q: Where do lumberjacks keep their pigs?

A: In their hog cabin.

Q: What is the difference between a football player and a dog?

A: A football player has a whole uniform, but a dog only pants.

Q: Why was the science teacher angry?

A: He was a mad scientist.

Q: Why was the tree excited about the future?

A: It was ready to turn over a new leaf.

Q: What do trees eat for breakfast?

A: Oakmeal.

Q: What is worse than finding a worm in your apple?

A: Finding *half* of a worm in your apple!

Q: Why did Cinderella get kicked out of the soccer game?

A: She ran away from the ball.

Q: What is a race car driver's favorite meal?

A: Fast food.

Q: What does a skipper eat for breakfast?

A: Captain Crunch.

Q: If April showers bring May flowers, what do Mayflowers bring?

A: Pilgrims.

Q: What runs around the football field but never moves?

A: A fence.

Q: Why was the jelly so stressed out?

A: It was spread too thin.

Awesome Animal Jokes

Q: A cowboy arrives at the ranch on a Sunday, stays three days, and leaves on Friday. How is that possible?

A: The horse's name is Friday.

Q: What do you call a bear standing in the rain?

A: A drizzly bear.

Q: What happened when the spider got a new car?

A: It took it for a spin.

Q: Why did the cow become an astronaut?

A: So it could walk on the moooo-n.

Q: Where do shrimp go if they need money?

A: The prawn shop.

Q: Why did the boy canary make the girl canary pay for her own meal on their date?

A: Because he was cheep.

Q: Why do flamingos stand on one leg?

A: If they lifted the other leg, they'd fall over.

Q: What do you get when you cross a fish and a kitten?

A: A purr-anha.

Q: How are fish and music the same?

A: They both have scales.

Q: What did the mother lion say to her cubs before dinner?

A: "Shall we prey?"

Q: What's worse than raining cats and dogs?

A: Hailing taxi cabs.

Q: Why are pigs so bad at football?

A: They're always hogging the ball.

Q: What do you call a lion whose car breaks down five miles before he gets to the zoo?

A: A cab.

Q: What is a whale's favorite game?

A: Swallow the leader.

Q: What do you call bears with no ears?

A: B.

Q: Why is it hard to trust what a baby chick is saying?

A: Talk is cheep.

Q: Why did the clown visit the aquarium?

A: To see the clown fish.

Q: What is the best way to communicate with a fish?

A: Drop it a line!

Q: Why couldn't the elephants go swimming at the pool?

A: They were always losing their trunks.

Q: Why did the sparrow go to the library?

A: It was looking for bookworms.

Q: What did the dog say when he rubbed sandpaper on his tail?

A: "Ruff, ruff."

Q: What kind of sea creature hates all the others?

A: A hermit crab.

Q: Where can you go to see mummies of cows?

A: The Mooseum of History.

Q: What kind of seafood tastes great with peanut butter?

A: Jellyfish.

Q: Why is it easy to play tricks on lollipops?

A: They're suckers.

Q: Why did the cat get detention at school?

A: Because he was a cheetah.

Q: Where do bees come from?

A: Stingapore and Beelivia.

Q: Why couldn't the polar bear get along with the penguin?

A: They were polar opposites.

Q: What did the rooster say to the hen?

A: "Don't count your chickens before they hatch."

Q: What happens when a cat eats a lemon?

A: You get a sourpuss.

Q: What language do pigs speak?

A: Swine language.

Q: What do cars and elephants have in common?

A: They both have trunks.

Q: What is a bat's motto?

A: Hang in there.

Q: What do you get when you cross a rabbit and frog?

A: A bunny ribbit.

Q: What do you get when you cross a dog and a daisy?

A: A collie-flower.

Q: What does a cat say when it's surprised?

A: "Me-WOW!"

Q: Why did the parakeet go to the candy store?

A: To get a tweet.

Q: **What do you have if your dog can't bark?**

A: A hush-puppy.

Q: **Why do seagulls fly over the sea?**

A: Because if they flew over the bay they'd be bagels.

Q: **Why did Rover beat up Fido?**

A: Because Rover was a Boxer.

Q: **What do you get when an elephant sneezes?**

A: You get out of the way!

Q: **What is the craziest bird in the world?**

A: The coo-coo bird.

Q: **What is the dumbest bird in the world?**

A: The do-do bird.

Q: **What do you get when your dog makes your breakfast?**

A: You get pooched eggs.

Q: **Why did the horse wake up with a headache?**

A: Because at bedtime he hit the hay.

Q: What do trees and dogs have in common?

A: They both have bark.

Q: What kind of bees never die?

A: Zom-bees.

Q: What do you call a lazy kangaroo?

A: A pouch potato.

Q: What happened when the sharks raced each other?

A: They tide (get it . . . they tied).

Q: Why couldn't the goats get along?

A: They kept butting heads.

Q: What type of bat is silly?

A: A ding-bat.

Q: When do fireflies get uptight?

A: When they need to lighten up.

Q: Why do rhinos have so many wrinkles?

A: Because they're so hard to iron.

Q: Where did the turtle fill up his gas tank?

A: At the shell station.

Q: Why did the pony get sent to his room without supper?

A: He wouldn't stop horsing around.

Q: What is a snake's favorite subject in school?

A: World hiss-tory.

Q: What kind of animal is related to a computer?

A: A ram.

Q: What do you call an insect that complains all the time?

A: A grumble-bee.

Q: Why were the deer, the chipmunk, and the squirrel laughing so hard?

A: Because the owl was a hoot!

Q: What do you call a monkey who won't behave?

A: A bad-boon.

Q: What kind of bugs read the dictionary?

A: Spelling bees.

Q: What do you call a calf that gets into trouble?

A: Grounded beef.

Q: What do you call a dinosaur who's scared all the time?

A: A nervous Rex.

Q: What do you call a polar bear in Hawaii?

A: Lost!

Q: Where do you take a sick bumblebee?

A: To the wasp-ital.

Q: Who made the fish's wishes come true?

A: Its fairy cod-mother.

Q: Where do pigs go for a rest?

A: To their ham-mock.

Q: What do you get if a cow is in an earthquake?

A: A milkshake.

Q: How does a farmer count his cattle?

A: With a cow-culator.

Q: Why does a milking stool only have three legs?

A: Because the cow has the udder one.

Q: Where do rabbits go after their wedding?

A: They go on their bunny-moon.

Joe: There were ten cats on a boat and one jumped off. How many were left?

Jack: I don't know, Joe. I guess nine?

Joe: No, there were none! They were all a bunch of copy cats.

Q: How come hyenas are so healthy?

A: Because laughter is the best medicine.

Q: Why don't Dalmatians like to take baths?

A: They don't like to be spotless.

Q: What do you get when sheep do karate?

A: Lamb chops.

Q: Why did the rooster go to the doctor?

A: It had the cock-a-doodle-flu.

Q: What do birds do before they work out?

A: They do their worm-ups.

Q: What kind of insects are bad at football?

A: Fumblebees.

Q: What do you call a deer with no eyes?

A: No eye deer (no idea).

Q: Why is it so easy for an elephant to get a job?

A: Because it will work for peanuts.

Q: What did the tiger say to her cubs when they wanted to go out and play?

A: "Be careful—it's a jungle out there!"

Q: Why did the monkey almost get fired?

A: It took him a while to get into the swing of things.

Q: Why is the snail one of the strongest creatures in the world?

A: It can carry its house on its back.

Q: What do you get when you cross a bear with a forest?

A: You get fur trees.

Q: Why did the elephant cross the road?

A: It's an elephant, so who's going to stop him?

Q: What is a frog's favorite flower?

A: A croak-us.

Q: How do you keep a dog from barking in the backseat of the car?

A: Put him in the front seat of the car.

Q: What do you get when you cross a monkey and a peach?

A: You get an ape-ricot.

Q: How do you greet a frog?

A: "Wart's up?"

Knock-Knock Jokes

Knock knock.
  Who's there?
Butter.
  Butter who?
**I butter not tell you—it's a
  secret.**

Knock knock.
  Who's there?
Wendy.
  Wendy who?
**Wendy you think we'll be
  done with these knock
  knock jokes?**

Knock knock.
  Who's there?
Hailey.
  Hailey who?
**Hailey a cab so I can go
  home.**

Knock knock.
  Who's there?
Wayne.
  Wayne who?
**The Wayne is really coming
  down, so open the door!**

Knock knock.
    Who's there?
Weasel.
    Weasel who?
Weasel be late if you don't
    hurry up.

Knock knock.
    Who's there?
Raymond.
    Raymond who?
Raymond me to go to the
    store to get some milk
    and eggs.

Knock knock.
    Who's there?
Nose.
    Nose who?
I nose a lot more knock
    knock jokes if you want
    to hear them.

Knock knock.
    Who's there?
Hannah.
    Hannah who?
Hannah me some of those
    apples, I'm hungry!

Knock knock.
    Who's there?
Little old lady.
    Little old lady who?
I didn't know you could
    yodel!

Knock knock.
    Who's there?
Olive.
    Olive who?
Olive you. Do you love me
    too?

Knock knock.
    Who's there?
Eileen.
    Eileen who?
I'm so tall, Eileen over to get
    through the door.

Knock knock.
    Who's there?
Les.
    Les who?
Les cut the small talk and let
    me in.

Knock knock.
> Who's there?

Brett.
> Brett who?

Brett you don't know who this is!

Knock knock.
> Who's there?

Bacon.
> Bacon who?

I'm bacon a cake for your birthday.

Knock knock.
> Who's there?

Irish.
> Irish who?

Irish you'd let me in.

Knock knock.
> Who's there?

Ashley.
> Ashley who?

Ashley I changed my mind, and I don't want to come in.

Knock knock.
> Who's there?

Italy.
> Italy who?

Italy a shame if you don't open this door!

Knock knock.
> Who's there?

Alda.
> Alda who?

Alda kids like my knock knock jokes.

Knock knock.
> Who's there?

Gwen.
> Gwen who?

Gwen do you think we can get together?

Knock knock.
> Who's there?

Francis.
> Francis who?

Francis next to Spain.

Knock knock.
> Who's there?

Cook.
> Cook who?

Are you as crazy as you
sound?

Knock knock.
> Who's there?

Juno.
> Juno who?

Juno it's me, so let me in
now!

Knock knock.
> Who's there?

Alex.
> Alex who?

Alex plain later, now let me
in!

Knock knock.
> Who's there?

Gladys.
> Gladys who?

Aren't you Gladys is the last
knock knock joke?

Knock knock.
> Who's there?

Joanna.
> Joanna who?

Joanna come out and play?

Knock knock.
> Who's there?

Archie.
> Archie who?

Archie going to let me in?

Knock knock.
> Who's there?

Robin.
> Robin who?

Robin a bank is against the
law.

Knock knock.
> Who's there?

Duncan.
> Duncan who?

Duncan cookies in milk
tastes good.

Knock knock.
　　Who's there?
Pastor.
　　Pastor who?
Pastor potatoes. I'm
　　hungry!

Knock knock.
　　Who's there?
Carson.
　　Carson who?
Carson the freeway drive
　　really fast.

Knock knock.
　　Who's there?
Ben.
　　Ben who?
I've Ben gone a lot lately
　　and came by to see you.

Knock knock.
　　Who's there?
Doug.
　　Doug who?
I Doug deep and still
　　couldn't find my keys.
　　Please let me in!

Knock knock.
　　Who's there?
Aldon.
　　Aldon who?
When you're Aldon with
　　dinner can you come
　　out and play?

Knock knock.
　　Who's there?
House.
　　House who?
House it going for you?

Knock knock.
　　Who's there?
Arlo.
　　Arlo who?
Arlo temperature is making
　　me cold. Please let me
　　in!

Knock knock.
　　Who's there?
Ben.
　　Ben who?
I haven't Ben over to visit in
　　a long time.

Knock knock.
    Who's there?
Mia.
    Mia who?
Mia hand is killing me from
    all this knocking. Will
    you please let me in?

Knock knock.
    Who's there?
Anna.
    Anna who?
Anna chance you'll let me
    in? It's cold out here!

Knock knock.
    Who's there?
Samantha.
    Samantha who?
Can you give me Samantha
    to my questions?

Knock knock.
    Who's there?
Lee.
    Lee who?
I'm lone Lee without you.
    Please let me in!

Knock knock.
    Who's there?
Ya.
    Ya who?
Giddyup, cowboy!

Knock knock.
    Who's there?
Cameron.
    Cameron who?
Is the Cameron? I want to
    take a picture.

Knock knock.
    Who's there?
Stan.
    Stan who?
Stan back because I'm going
    to break down the door!

Knock knock.
    Who's there?
Ice.
    Ice who?
It would be really ice to see
    you, so please open the
    door.

Knock knock.
Who's there?
Eyes.
Eyes who?
Eyes better come in before I
catch a cold.

Knock knock.
Who's there?
Ada.
Ada who?
I Ada lot for lunch, so now
I'm really full.

Knock knock.
Who's there?
Dewey.
Dewey who?
Dewey have to go to school
today?

Knock knock.
Who's there?
Peas.
Peas who?
Peas, can you come out and
play?

Knock knock.
Who's there?
Fanny.
Fanny who?
If Fanny body asks, I'm not
home.

Knock knock.
Who's there?
Hugo.
Hugo who?
Hugo first and I'll go
second.

Knock knock.
Who's there?
Megan.
Megan who?
You're Megan me crazy with
all of these knock knock
jokes.

Knock knock.
Who's there?
Owen.
Owen who?
I'm Owen you a lot of
money, but I'll pay you
back soon!

Knock knock.
Who's there?
Lucas.
Lucas who?
Lucas in the eye and tell us you don't want to hear another knock knock joke!

Knock knock.
Who's there?
Luke.
Luke who?
You Luke like you want to hear another knock knock joke!

Knock knock.
Who's there?
Quack.
Quack who?
You quack me up with all these knock knock jokes.

Knock knock.
Who's there?
Sadie.
Sadie who?
If I Sadie magic word will you let me in?

Knock knock.
Who's there?
Queen.
Queen who?
I had a bath, so I'm queen as a whistle!

Knock knock.
Who's there?
Baby Al.
Baby Al who?
Baby Al will, baby Al won't.

Knock knock.
Who's there?
Canoe.
Canoe who?
Canoe come out and play?

Knock knock.
  Who's there?
Oldest.
  Oldest who?
Oldest knocking is giving
  me a headache.

Knock knock.
  Who's there?
Woody.
  Woody who?
Woody like to hear another
  knock knock joke?

Knock knock.
  Who's there?
B.C.
  B.C. who?
I'll B.C.-ing you soon.

Knock knock.
  Who's there?
Weed.
  Weed who?
Weed better go home now
  for dinner.

Knock knock.
  Who's there?
Dawn.
  Dawn who?
Dawn mess around, or I'm
  leaving!

Knock knock.
  Who's there?
Rockefeller.
  Rockefeller who?
Rockefeller in his cradle,
  and he'll go right to
  sleep.

Knock knock.
  Who's there?
Dora.
  Dora who?
A Dora is between us, so
  open up!

Knock knock.
  Who's there?
Braden.
  Braden who?
Are you busy Braden your
  hair, or will you open
  the door?

Knock knock.
  Who's there?
Hannah.
  Hannah who?
Hannah over the keys so I
  can open this door!

Knock knock.
  Who's there?
Gary.
  Gary who?
Gary me inside—my legs
  are tired.

Knock knock.
  Who's there?
I don't know.
  I don't know who?
I don't know who either, so
  open the door and find
  out.

Knock knock.
  Who's there?
Beth.
  Beth who?
I didn't sneeze!

Knock knock.
  Who's there?
Shelby.
  Shelby who?
Shelby coming around the
  mountain when she
  comes!

Knock knock.
  Who's there?
Howl.
  Howl who?
Howl we get away from
  all these knock knock
  jokes?

Knock knock.
  Who's there?
Water.
  Water who?
Water you doing at my
  house?

Knock knock.
  Who's there?
Vera.
  Vera who?
Vera few people think these
  jokes are funny.

Knock knock.
Who's there?
Garden.
Garden who?
Stop garden the door and let
me in!

Knock knock.
Who's there?
Annie.
Annie who?
Annie reason you're not
opening the door?

Knock knock.
Who's there?
Dozen.
Dozen who?
Dozen anyone ever open the
door?

Knock knock.
Who's there?
Dragon.
Dragon who?
These jokes are dragon on
and on.

Knock knock.
Who's there?
Willie.
Willie who?
Willie tell us more knock
knock jokes?

Knock knock.
Who's there?
Moe.
Moe who?
Moe knock knock jokes,
please.

Knock knock.
Who's there?
Ernest.
Ernest who?
Ernest is full of chicken
eggs.

Knock knock.
Who's there?
Taylor.
Taylor who?
Taylor brother to pick up
his toys.

Knock knock.
  Who's there?
Dewy.
  Dewy who?
Dewy get to hear more
  knock knock jokes?

Knock knock.
  Who's there?
Lettuce.
  Lettuce who?
Lettuce in and you'll find
  out.

Knock knock.
  Who's there?
Collette.
  Collette who?
Collette crazy, but I'd like to
  come in and see you.

Knock knock.
  Who's there?
Achoo.
  Achoo who?
Achoo my gum every day.

Knock knock.
  Who's there?
Juicy.
  Juicy who?
Juicy any monsters under
  my bed?

Knock knock.
  Who's there?
Alaska.
  Alaska who?
Alaska one more time to let
  me in!

Knock knock.
  Who's there?
Yellow.
  Yellow who?
Yellow, and how are you
  doing today?

Knock knock.
  Who's there?
Handsome.
  Handsome who?
Handsome food to me—I'm
  really hungry!

Knock knock.
  Who's there?
Rabbit.
  Rabbit who?
Rabbit carefully, it's a
  Christmas present!

Knock knock.
  Who's there?
Sarah.
  Sarah who?
Is Sarah doctor in the
  house? I feel sick!

Knock knock.
  Who's there?
Ida.
  Ida who?
Ida know, why don't you
  open up and find out?

Knock knock.
  Who's there?
Oscar.
  Oscar who?
Oscar a silly question, get a
  silly answer.

Knock knock.
  Who's there?
Dishes.
  Dishes who?
Dishes not the end of my
  knock knock jokes!

Knock knock.
  Who's there?
Olive.
  Olive who?
Olive these knock knock
  jokes are making me
  sick.

Knock knock.
  Who's there?
Who.
  Who who?
Are you an owl or
  something?

Knock knock.
  Who's there?
Sombrero.
  Sombrero who?
Sombrero-ver the rainbow.

Knock knock.
Who's there?
Ken.
Ken who?
Ken you come out and play?

Knock knock.
Who's there?
Itchy.
Itchy who?
Bless you!

Knock knock.
Who's there?
Ivan.
Ivan who?
Ivan to come in, so please open the door!

Knock knock.
Who's there?
Dwayne.
Dwayne who?
Dwayne the bathtub! I'm drowning!

Knock knock.
Who's there?
Walter.
Walter who?
Walter you doing here so early?

Knock knock.
Who's there?
Justin.
Justin who?
You're Justin time for dinner.

Knock knock.
Who's there?
Wanda.
Wanda who?
Do you Wanda let me in yet?

Knock knock.
Who's there?
Everest.
Everest who?
Do we Everest from telling knock knock jokes?

Knock knock.
  Who's there?
Bill Gates.
  Bill Gates who?
Bill Gates a bike for his
  birthday.

Knock knock.
  Who's there?
Lion.
  Lion who?
Quit lion around and open
  the door.

Knock knock.
  Who's there?
Paws.
  Paws who?
Can you paws for a moment
  and open the door?

Knock knock.
  Who's there?
Zoo.
  Zoo who?
Zoo think you can come out
  and play?

Knock knock.
  Who's there?
Tide.
  Tide who?
Are you Tide of knock
  knock jokes yet?

Knock knock.
  Who's there?
Candace.
  Candace who?
Candace be the last knock
  knock joke?

Knock knock.
  Who's there?
Shirley.
  Shirley who?
Shirley I'll tell you another
  knock knock joke.

Knock knock.
  Who's there?
Aspen.
  Aspen who?
Aspen thinking about you
  all day.

Knock knock.
Who's there?
Bonnie.
Bonnie who?
It's Bonnie long time since
I've seen you.

Knock knock.
Who's there?
Andy.
Andy who?
Andy-body want to go to the
movies?

Knock knock.
Who's there?
Isabel.
Isabel who?
Isabel ringing or am I just
hearing things?

Knock knock.
Who's there?
Benjamin.
Benjamin who?
I've Benjamin to the music
all day.

Knock knock.
Who's there?
Bailey.
Bailey who?
I know you Bailey know me,
but can I come in?

Knock knock.
Who's there?
Byron.
Byron who?
There's a Byron get one free
sale at the mall!

Knock knock.
Who's there?
Les.
Les who?
Les one there is a rotten
egg!

Knock knock.
Who's there?
Baldwin.
Baldwin who?
You'll be Baldwin you're
older.

Knock knock.
  Who's there?
Barry.
  Barry who?
Let's Barry the hatchet and
  be friends again.

Knock knock.
  Who's there?
Carrie.
  Carrie who?
Will you Carrie my books
  for me?

Knock knock.
  Who's there?
Calvin.
  Calvin who?
Calvin you get there so I
  know that you made it
  safely.

Knock knock.
  Who's there?
Colin.
  Colin who?
Just Colin to tell you
  another great knock
  knock joke.

Knock knock.
  Who's there?
Orange.
  Orange who?
Orange you glad it's me?

Knock knock.
  Who's there?
Conner.
  Conner who?
Conner brother come out
  and play?

Knock knock.
  Who's there?
Jim.
  Jim who?
Jim mind if I come in and
  stay awhile?

Knock knock.
  Who's there?
Mike.
  Mike who?
Turn up the Mike so I can
  hear you better.

Tongue Twisters

Try to Say These Ten Times Fast

Giggly gladiator.

Fresh French fries.

Selfish shellfish.

Sock, skirt, shirt.

Snatch stacked snacks.

Cheap cheese stinks.

Goofy gorillas gobble grapefruits.

Tall trees toss leaves.

Purple penguins pick pickles.

Cooked cookies crumble quickly.

Soggy stuff smells suspicious.

Big bad bears blow blue bubbles.

Tasty tomato tostadas.

You'll push she'll push.

Six slimy snails sailed silently.

Anonymous

A big black bug bit a big black dog
on his big black nose!

Kitty Morrow

Tongue Twisting Poems

Billy Button

Billy Button bought a buttered biscuit.
Did Billy Button buy a buttered biscuit?
If Billy Button bought a buttered biscuit,
Where's the buttered biscuit Billy Button bought?

Shirish Karker

A Fly and a Flea in a Flue

A fly and a flea in a flue
Were imprisoned, so what could they do?
Said the fly, "Let us flee!"
"Let us fly!" said the flea,
So they flew through a flaw in the flue.

Ogden Nash

Some Things
to Think About

What do you call a male ladybug?

Why don't they call moustaches mouthbrows?

Why doesn't glue stick to the inside of the bottle?

What do they call their good plates in China?

Why is a boxing ring square?

If a fly didn't have wings, would we call it a walk?

Do fish ever get thirsty?

2

LAUGH
-OUT-
LOUD
ANIMAL
JOKES
for
KIDS

Q: Where do ants like to eat?

A: At a restaur-ant.

Q: What do alligators drink after they work out?

A: Gator-ade.

Q: What do a mouse and a wheel have in common?

A: They both squeak.

Q: What do frogs use so they can see better?

A: Frog-lights.

Q: Why can't you trust a pig?

A: It will always squeal on you.

Q: What kind of dog cries the most?

A: A Chi-wah-wah (Chihuahua).

Q: Where do birds invest their money?

A: In the stork market (stock market).

Q: Why can't you borrow money from a canary?

A: Because they're so cheep (cheap).

Q: What happened to the bee after he had four cups of coffee?

A: He got a buzz.

Q: Why was the bird nervous after lunch?

A: He had butterflies in his stomach.

Q: What did the father buffalo say to his son as he left for school?

A: "Bison (Bye, Son)."

Q: Where did the bat go to get some money?

A: The blood bank.

Q: What kind of bear doesn't have any teeth?

A: A gummy bear.

Q: What do you get from a pampered cow?

A: Spoiled milk.

Q: How did the cow make some extra money?

A: By mooooo-nlighting at another farm.

Q: Why did the cow become an astronaut?

A: So it could walk on the moooo-n.

Q: What do cows like to eat?

A: Smoooothies.

> ## Did You Know . . .
>
> • Cows give an average of 2,000 gallons of milk per year. That's over 30,000 glasses of milk!
>
> www.arsusda.gov
>
> • There are about 11 million cows in America. They will make about 57.5 billion gallons of milk in a year.
>
> www.umpquadairy.com

Q: Why were the chickens so tired?

A: They were working around the cluck.

Q: What animals do you find in a monastery?

A: Chip-monks!

A duck walks into a store and asks the manager if he sells grapes. The manager says no, so the duck leaves. The next day the duck goes back to the store and asks the manager if he sells grapes. The manager says, "NO, we don't sell grapes," so the duck leaves the store. The next day the duck goes back to the same store and asks the manager if he sells grapes. The manager is furious now and says, "NO, WE DO NOT SELL GRAPES! IF YOU COME BACK AND ASK IF WE SELL GRAPES AGAIN, I'LL GLUE YOUR BEAK TO THE FLOOR!" The next day the duck goes back to the same store and says to the manager, "Excuse me, do you sell glue at this store?" The manager says, "No, we don't sell glue." The duck replies, "That's good. Do you sell grapes?"

Joe: **Did that dolphin splash you by accident?**

Bill: No, it was on porpoise!

Q: Where did the toy giraffe go when it was broken?

A: To get plastic surgery.

Q: What do you give a pig that has a cold?

A: Trough syrup!

Q: Why did the porcupine get sent home from the party?

A: He was popping all the balloons!

Q: What do you get when you cross a pig with a Christmas tree?

A: A pork-u-pine.

Q: What is a reptile's favorite movie?

A: The Lizard of Oz.

Q: Why did the snake lose his case in court?

A: He didn't have a leg to stand on.

Q: What kind of bull doesn't have horns?

A: A bullfrog.

Q: Why did the skunk have to stay in bed and take its medicine?

A: It was the doctor's odors.

Did You Know . . .

A shrimp's heart is located in its head.

Q: Why are fish so bad at basketball?

A: They don't like getting close to the net.

Q: Where do dogs go if they lose their tails?

A: The re-tail store.

Q: What are the funniest fish at the aquarium?

A: The clown fish.

Q: What is as big as an elephant but weighs zero pounds?

A: An elephant's shadow.

Q: Why are horses always so negative?

A: They say "neigh" (nay) to everything.

Q: What is black and white, black and white, black and white, black and white, splash?

A: A penguin rolling down an iceberg into the water.

Q: What is the smartest animal?

A: A snake, because no one can pull its leg.

Two men went deer hunting. One man asked the other, "Did you ever hunt bear?" The other hunter said, "No, but one time I went fishing in my shorts."

Q: Why did the robin go to the library?

A: It was looking for bookworms.

Q: What is black and white and red all over?

A: A penguin that's embarrassed.

Q: What do you call a pig that is no fun to be around?

A: A boar.

Q: What kind of fish can perform surgery?

A: Sturgeons.

Q: What do cats like to put in their milk?

A: Mice cubes.

Q: What do you get when you cross an elephant with a fish?

A: Swimming trunks.

Q: What do you do if your dog steals your spelling homework?

A: Take the words right out of his mouth.

Q: What did the whale say to the dolphin?

A: "Long time no sea (see)."

Q: What sound do porcupines make when they kiss?

A: Ouch!

Q: What happened when the frog's car broke down?

A: It had to be toad away (towed).

Q: What is a whale's favorite candy?

A: Blubber gum.

Q: What do you get when you cross a cow and a rabbit?

A: You get hare in your milk.

Q: Why did the horse keep falling over?

A: It just wasn't stable.

Q: How do fish pay their bills?

A: With sand-dollars.

Q: Which creatures on Noah's ark didn't come in pairs?

A: The worms—they came in apples.

Q: What kind of animal do you take into battle?

A: An army-dillo.

Did You Know . . .
Penguins can jump up to 6 feet high.

Q: What kind of bird likes to make bread?

A: The do-do bird (dough-dough).

Q: What do you get if you mix a rabbit and a snake?

A: A jump rope.

Q: **How do you shoot a bumblebee?**

A: With a bee-bee gun.

What Does the Bee Do?

What does the bee do?
Bring home honey.
And what does Father do?
Bring home money.
And what does Mother do?
Lay out the money.
And what does the baby do?
Eat up the honey.

Christina Rosetti

Q: **Why do bumblebees smell so good?**

A: They always wear bee-odorant.

Q: **Why was the Tyrannosaurus rex so boring?**

A: He was a dino-snore.

Q: **What is a frog's favorite drink?**

A: Croak-a-Cola.

Q: **What is the scariest kind of bug?**

A: A zom-bee (zombie).

Q: Why are frogs so happy?

A: They just eat whatever bugs them!

Q: What is the difference between a fish and a piano?

A: You can't tuna fish (tune a fish).

Q: What did the horse say when he tripped and fell down?

A: "Help! I've fallen and I can't giddy-up!"

Q: If people like sandwiches, what do lions like?

A: Man-wiches.

Q: Why did the chicken cross the road?

A: To show the squirrel it could be done.

Q: Why did the turkey cross the road?

A: To prove it wasn't a chicken.

Q: What do you give a horse with a bad cold?

A: Cough stirrup.

Q: Who falls asleep at a bullfight?

A: A bull-dozer.

Q: Why did the cat and her kittens clean up their mess?

A: They didn't want to litter.

Q: What is a sheep's favorite kind of food?

A: Bah-bah-cue.

Q: What is a hyena's favorite kind of candy?

A: A Snickers bar.

Q: How do sea creatures communicate under water?

A: With shell phones.

Q: Why was the dog depressed?

A: Because his life was so ruff.

Q: What does a rabbit use to fix its fur?

A: Hare-spray.

Q: What kind of insect is hard to understand?

A: A mumble-bee.

Q: What do you call a cow that can't give milk?

A: A milk dud.

Q: Why did the chickens get in trouble at school?

A: They were using fowl language.

Q: Where does a lizard keep his groceries?

A: In the refriger-gator.

Q: Why is talking to cows a waste of time?

A: Whatever you say goes in one ear and out the udder.

Q: What do you get when you cross a dog with a cell phone?

A: A golden receiver.

Q: Where did the bull take the cow on a date?

A: To dinner and a mooovie.

Q: What is the world's hungriest animal?

A: A turkey—it just gobble, gobble, gobbles!

Q: What happened to the mouse when it fell in the bathtub?

A: It came out squeaky clean.

Q: Why did the cowboy ask his cattle so many questions?

A: He wanted to grill them.

Q: What is a duck's favorite snack?

A: Cheese and quackers.

Q: What do you call a cow that's afraid of everything?

A: A cow-ard.

Q: What is the difference between a cat and a frog?

A: A cat has nine lives, but a frog croaks every day.

Q: What does a frog say when he washes windows?

A: "Rubbit, rubbit, rubbit."

Q: What do you get when a lion escapes from the zoo?

A: A cat-astrophe.

Q: What is the best kind of cat to have around?

A: A dandy-lion.

Q: Where do trout keep their money?

A: In a river bank.

Q: What did the worm say to her daughter when she came home late?

A: "Where on earth have you been?"

Q: What did the boy say when he threw a slug across the room?

A: "Man, how slime flies!"

Q: What do you get when you cross Bambi with an umbrella?

A: You get a rain-deer (reindeer).

Q: Who brings kittens for Christmas?

A: Santa Claws.

Q: What did Santa give Rudolph for his upset stomach?

A: Elk-A-Seltzer.

Q: Why can't an elephant's trunk be 12 inches long?

A: Because then it would be a a foot.

Q: What do you get when you cross a fish and a tree branch?

A: A fish stick.

Q: What kind of bird is always depressed?

A: A bluebird.

Q: How high can a bumblebee count?

A: To a buzz-illion.

Q: Why are oysters so strong?

A: Because of their mussels (muscles).

Q: What do you get when you throw a pony in the ocean?

A: A seahorse!

Q: What is the most colorful kind of snake in the world?

A: A rain-boa constrictor (rainbow).

Q: What does a cow keep in its wallet?

A: Moo-la.

Q: What kind of fish comes out at night?

A: A starfish.

Q: What did the dog say to its owner?

A: "I woof you."

Q: Why couldn't the dog visit the psychiatrist?

A: Because it wasn't allowed on the couch.

Q: What kind of cats like to play in the water?

A: Sea lions.

Knock knock!
Who's there?
Moo.
Moo, who?
Make up your mind—are you a cow or an owl?

Q: How does a dog say goodbye?

A: "Bone-Voyage!"

Q: What do llamas like to drink?

A: Strawberry llama-nade (lemonade).

Q: What do you call a fish with no eyes?

A: Fsh!

Q: What do you get when you throw a pig into the bushes?

A: A hedge-hog.

Q: What did the duck say to the clerk at the store?

A: "Just put it on my bill!"

Q: What did the frogs say to each other on their wedding day?

A: "I'll love you until the day I croak!"

Where Do Animals Come From?

Bees come from Stingapore
Cows come from Moo-rocco
Fish come from Wales
Sharks come from Finland
Ants come from Frants (France)
Dogs come from Bark-celona
   (Barcelona)
Pigs come from New Ham-shire
Chickens come from Turkey
Cats come from Purrr-u (Peru)
Birds come from Air-azona
Sheep come from the Baa-hamas
Snakes come from Hississippi

Q: Why was the golden retriever so stressed out?

A: Because he has so doggone much to do.

Q: Why was the horse in so much pain?

A: Because he was a charlie horse.

Q: What is red and weights 14,000 pounds?

A: An elephant holding its breath.

Q: What do cats like to eat for a snack?

A: Mice krispy bars.

Did You Know . . .

A hedgehog's heart beats 300 times per minute.

Q: How did the bunny rabbit feel when he ran out of carrots?

A: It made him unhoppy!

Q: What does a hen do when she goes grocery shopping?

A: She makes a list and chicks it twice!

Q: What did the fish say when it won the prize?

A: "That's fin-tastic (fantastic)!"

Q: Why did the grizzly tell the same story over and over?

A: Because he said it *bears* repeating!

Q: What will a moose do if he calls when you're not home?

A: He'll leave a detailed moose-age.

Q: What do you get when you put glasses on a pony?

A: A see-horse.

Q: Where to bunnies like to eat?

A: IHOP!

Q: How do you know when a rhino is ready to charge?

A: It gets out its credit card.

Knock knock!
     Who's there?
Raymond.
     Raymond who?
Raymond me to take the dog for a walk!

Q: What do you call a racoon that crosses the road with his eyes shut?

A: Roadkill!

Q: Where should a 600-pound lion go?

A: On a diet!

Q: How do you keep a skunk from smelling?

A: Hold its nose!

Did You Know . . .

A butterfly's tastebuds are in its feet.

Q: What do you get when you cross a bear with a skunk?

A: Winnie the Pew.

Q: What kind of sea creature is always depressed?

A: A blue whale.

Q: What did the beaver say to the tree?

A: "It's been nice getting to *gnaw* you!"

Q: What did the roach wear to the party?

A: A cockbroach.

Q: Why was the dog hungry all the time?

A: Because it was a chow.

Q: What kind of animal wears shoes while it's sleeping?

A: A horse!

Q: Why did the gum cross the road?

A: Because it was stuck to the chicken's shoe!

Q: How does a mother hen know when her chicks are ready to hatch?

A: She uses an egg timer.

Q: What happens when you get a thousand bunnies to line up and jump backwards?

A: You have a receding hare line!

Q: Where is the best place to park your dog?

A: The barking lot.

Q: What do you get when a cat climbs down your chimney with a bag of presents?

A: Santa Paws.

Q: Why can't you hear a dinosaur talk?

A: Because dinosaurs are extinct!

Q: Why don't lobsters share their toys?

A: Because they're shellfish (selfish)!

Knock knock!
     Who's there?
Either.
     Either who?
It's the Either Bunny!

Q: What is a chicken's favorite composer?

A: Bach, Bach, Bach!

Q: What is a fly's favorite composer?

A: Shoo-bert (Schubert).

Q: What do you get when you cross a bat and a cell phone?

A: A bat-mobile.

Q: Did you know that a kangaroo can jump higher than your house?

A: Of course! Your house can't jump!

Q: What time does a duck get up?

A: At the quack of dawn.

Q: What is black, white, and wet all over?

A: A zebra that was pushed into a swimming pool!

Q: What's black, white, and laughing?

A: The zebra that pushed the other zebra into the swimming pool!

Q: Why don't bunnies tell scary stories?

A: Because it makes the hare stand up on the back of their necks.

Q: What do you call a man with a seagull on his head?

A: Cliff.

Q: What do you call a monkey in a minefield?

A: A ba-BOOM!

Q: What do you call a pig that took a plane?

A: Swine flew (flu).

Q: What was the elephant doing on the freeway?

A: I don't know—about 10 miles per hour?

Jack: Do you like that cow over there?

Jill: No, I like the udder one!

Q: What do cats use to do their homework?

A: A meow-culator.

Did You Know . . .

The chow is the only dog that does not have a pink tongue.

Q: Why did the hornet have to fly back home?

A: Because he forgot his yellow jacket.

Q: Why did the bee visit the barber?

A: Because he wanted a buzz cut.

Bill: Would you like some honey?

Bob: May-bee!

Q: How did the bee get ready for school?

A: She used her honey comb!

Q: What do you get when you cross a vulture and a bumblebee?

A: A buzz-ard.

Q: What is a horse's favorite kind of fruit?

A: Straw-berries.

Q: What is a horse's favorite kind of nut?

A: Hay-zelnuts.

Q: What is a mouse's favorite game?

A: Hide and squeak.

Q: Why do birds fly south for the winter?

A: Because it's too far to walk, and their feet won't reach the pedals on a bicycle!

Cow #1: Did you hear about that crazy disease going around called mad cow disease?

Cow #2: I sure did—good thing I'm a penguin!

A policeman saw a lady with a hippopotamus walking down the street. He said, "Ma'am, you need to take that hippo to the zoo." The next day the lady was again walking down the street with the hippopotamus. The policeman said, "Ma'am, I told you to take that hippo to the zoo." The lady replied, "I did take him to the zoo, and today I'm taking him to the movies!"

Q: What is the best way to communicate with a squirrel?

A: Climb up a tree and act like a nut!

Q: Why can't cats drink milk in outer space?

A: Because the milk is in flying saucers!

Q: What's more annoying than a cat meowing outside your bedroom window?

A: *Ten* cats meowing outside your bedroom window!

Q: What do you do when you come upon two snails fighting?

A: Just let them slug it out . . .

Did You Know . . .

An ostrich's eye is bigger than its brain.

Q: What's the best way to learn about spiders?

A: On a web-site!

Q: What does a frog drink when it wants to lose weight?

A: Diet Croak.

Q: Why did the firefly get bad grades on his report card?

A: Because he wasn't very bright!

Q: Why was the caterpillar running for its life?

A: Because it was being chased by a dog-erpillar!

The Caterpillar

Caterpillar
Brown and furry
Caterpillar in a hurry,
Take a walk
To the shady lead, or stalk,
Or what not,
Which may be the chosen spot.
No toad spy you,
Hovering bird of prey pass by you;
Spin and die,
To live again a butterfly.

Christina Rosetti

Q: What do you get when you cross a dog and a snowman?

A: Frostbite.

Q: What is the difference between a fly and an eagle?

A: An eagle can fly, but a fly can't eagle.

Q: **When is it bad luck to see a black cat?**

A: When you're a mouse!

A duck went shopping at the grocery story and went to the register to pay. The store clerk asked, "Don't you have exact change" The duck answered, "Nope, sorry, I only carry bills!"

Q: **What do you call an elephant that never takes a bath?**

A: A smell-ephant!

Q: **What is a fish's favorite game show?**

A: Name that tuna (tune).

Knock knock!
    Who's there?
Bee.
    Bee who?
Just bee yourself!

Knock knock!
Who's there?
Owl.
Owl who?
Owl tell you another joke if you let me in . . .

Knock knock!
Who's there?
Aardvark.
Aardvark who?
Aardvark a thousand miles just to see you!

Knock knock!
Who's there?
Amos.
Amos who?
Ouch! Amos-quito bit me!

Knock knock!
Who's there?
Bug spray.
Bug spray who?
Bug spray they won't get squished!

Q: Where do horses live?
A: In neigh-borhoods.

Q: What kind of fish are worth a lot of money?

A: Goldfish.

Q: Where do monkeys make their burgers?

A: On the grill-a (gorilla).

Q: What did one nightcrawler say to the other nightcrawler?

A: "I know this great place down the road where we can eat dirt cheap!"

Q: Why does a herd of deer have plenty of money?

A: Because they have a lot of bucks!

Did You Know . . .

An owl can't move its eyeballs.

Q: What is a bug's favorite music?

A: The Beatles.

Q: What is a frogs favorite outdoor game?

A: Croak-quet (croquet).

Q: What kind of animal will never leave you alone?

A: The badger.

Q: Why did the bug get up early every morning?

A: Because it was a praying mantis.

Q: What kind of animal always contradicts itself?

A: A hippo-crite.

Q: Where do you put your dog when he's not behaving?

A: In the grrrrrage!

Q: What do you call a cat with eight legs that can swim?

A: An octo-puss.

Q: Why were the robins eating cake?

A: Because it was their bird-thday!

Q: Why did the pythons decide to get married?

A: Because they had a crush on each other.

Q: What do you do if there is a lion in your bed?

A: Go to a hotel for the night!

Q: What do you get when you cross a snail and a porcupine?

A: A slow poke.

Q: What's green, has six legs, and climbs bean stalks?

A: The Jolly Green Gi-ant.

Q: What's grey and goes round and round and round?

A: An elephant on a merry-go-round.

Q: Why did the racoon cross the road twice?

A: Because it was a double crosser.

Q: What do you get when you have a bunch of giraffes on the highway?

A: A giraffic jam.

Q: What performs at the circus and flies around eating mosquitos?

A: An acro-bat.

Q: Why was the crow on the phone?

A: Because he was making a long distance phone caw!

Customer: Do you serve turkeys here?

Waitress: We serve anyone, so go ahead and take a seat.

Q: How do fleas travel from dog to dog?

A: By *itch* hiking.

Knock knock!
　Who's there?
Gnat.
　Gnat who?
I'm *gnat* who you think I am!

Knock knock!
　Who's there?
Moose.
　Moose who?
It *moose* be time to let me in, so open the door!

Q: **How do you know which end of a worm is the head?**

A: Tickle the middle and see which end laughs.

Q: **Why are chickens so bad at baseball?**

A: Because they're always hitting fowl balls.

Q: **What do you get when you cross a beetle and a rabbit?**

A: Bugs bunny!

Q: **What do skunks like to eat when they're hungry?**

A: Peanut butter and smelly sandwiches.

Q: **What do you get when you cross a penguin and a jalapeño?**

A: A chilly pepper.

Q: Why can't you trust what a pig says?

A: Because it's full of bologna.

Q: What's large, gray, and has eighteen wheels?

A: An elephant in a semi-truck.

Q: What is a polar bear's favorite breakfast?

A: Ice krispies.

Q: Why did all the animals fall asleep in the barn?

A: Because the pigs were so boar-ing (boring).

Q: Why didn't the snake know how much it weighed?

A: Because it shed its scales.

Q: What does a leopard say after dinner?

A: "That hit the spot!"

Did You Know . . .

A bat lives about 40 years.

Q: How does a cow get to church on Sunday?

A: On its moo-tercycle.

Q: Why did the moose lift weights at the gym?

A: Because it wanted big moose-les (muscles).

Q: Why didn't the crab spend any of his money?

A: Because he was a penny pincher.

Q: What does a cow like to drink before bed?

A: De-calf-inated coffee (decaffeinated).

Q: What are you doing if you're staring at a starfish?

A: Stargazing.

Q: Why was the duck happy after his doctor appointment?

A: Because he got a clean bill of health.

Q: Where do bugs go to do their shopping?

A: The flea market.

Q: What kind of dessert do dogs run away from?

A: Pound cake.

Q: How do you know if there is a black bear in your oven?

A: The oven door won't close!

Q: Why did the cheetah get glasses?

A: Because it was seeing spots.

Knock knock!
Who's there?
Cod.
Cod who?
Cod **you let me in? It's cold out here!**

Knock knock!
Who's there?
Shellfish.
Shellfish who?
Don't be shellfish—let me in!

Knock knock!
Who's there?
Rhino.
Rhino who?
Rhino you want to let me in.

Knock knock!
Who's there?
Raven.
Raven who?
I've been *raven* about you to all my friends, so won't you let me in?

Q: What is the richest bird in the world?

A: The golden eagle.

Q: Why was a pig on the airplane?

A: Because its owner wanted to see pigs fly.

Q: Why was the frog in a bad mood?

A: Because he was having a toad-ally bad day.

Q: What do you call an elephant in a phone booth?

A: Stuck!

Q: Why were the elephants kicked off the beach?

A: Because they kept throwing their trunks in the water.

Q: Where do old ants go?

A: The ant-ique store.

Q: What do you get when you cross a cow and a toad?

A: A bullfrog.

Q: What do you get when you cross a water buffalo and a chicken?

A: Soggy buffalo wings.

Q: **How do chickens stay in shape?**

A: They eggs-ercise.

Q: **How do skunks watch the news?**

A: On their smellevision.

Q: **Why did the rabbit work at the hotel?**

A: Because he made a good bellhop.

Josh: **How do you know carrots are good for your eyes?**

Anna: Have you ever seen a rabbit wearing glasses?

Q: **What do dinosaurs put in their cars?**

A: Fossil fuel.

Q: **How did the pig write a letter?**

A: With its pig pen.

Did You Know . . .

An ant can lift 20 times its own body weight.

What's Their Motto?

Bee: Mind your own beeswax.

Bear: Grin and bear it.

Cow: Keep mooooooving.

Dog: Don't bark up the wrong tree.

Owl: It's not what you know, it's WHO you know.

Rabbit: Don't worry, be hoppy.

Cat: Don't litter.

Mouse: The squeaky wheel gets the grease.

Bat: Just *fang* in there.

Otter: Do unto *otters* as you would have them do unto you.

Robin: The early bird gets the worm.

Fox: Don't count your chickens before they're hatched.

Fish: Absence makes the heart grow flounder.

Q: What happened to the snake when it got upset?

A: It got hiss-terical.

Q: What did the rattlesnakes do after they had a fight?

A: They hissed and made up.

Did You Know . . .

The king cobra can grow to over 18 feet long. It's the largest poisonous snake in the world. Just a small amount of its venom can kill up to 30 people.

Q: What does a monkey drink with its breakfast?

A: Ape juice.

Q: What happened to the platypus when it fell in the hole?

A: It became a *splat*ypus.

Q: How do crocodiles make their dinner?

A: In a croc pot.

Q: Where do ants go when it's hot outside?
A: Ant-arctica.

Q: Why do pigs make great comedians?
A: Because they like to ham it up.

Q: What is a pig's favorite play?
A: Hamlet.

Q: Where do pigs put their dirty laundry?
A: In the hamper.

Q: Why was the pig having trouble walking?
A: Because he pulled his hamstring.

Q: What do you get if you cross a dog and a mosquito?
A: A bloodhound.

Did You Know . . .

The duckbill platypus can store over 500 worms in its cheeks.

Q: What do you get when you combine a cat and a dog?

A: Cat nip.

Q: What does a squirrel like to eat for breakfast?

A: Dough-nuts!

Q: What is a monkey's favorite book?

A: Apes of Wrath.

Q: How do skunks get in touch with each other?

A: They use their smell phones.

Q: How do crabs call each other?

A: They use their shell phones.

Q: What do you call a ladybug that won't clean up its room?

A: A litter bug.

Knock knock!
    Who's there?
Otter.
    Otter who?
You otter open this door and let me in!

Knock knock!
Who's there?
Dragon.
Dragon who?
Quit dragon this out and open the door!

Q: **What happened to the rich snake who had everything?**

A: He decided to scale back.

Q: **How do you stop a 10-pound parrot from talking too much?**

A: Buy a 20-pound cat?

Q: **Why did the cat study its spelling words fifty times?**

A: Because practice makes purr-fect.

At The Zoo

First I saw the white bear, then I saw the black;
Then I saw the camel with a hump upon his back;
Then I saw the grey wolf, with mutton in his maw;
Then I saw the wombat waddle in the straw;
Then I saw the elephant a-waving of his trunk;
Then I saw the monkeys—mercy, how unpleasantly
  they smelt!

William Makepeace Thackeray

Q: What do you get when you cross a brontosaurus and a lemon?

A: A dino-sour.

Q: What's green, has warts, and lives alone?

A: Hermit the frog.

Q: Why was the bird wearing a wig?

A: Because it was a bald eagle.

Q: What did the baby shark do when it got lost in the ocean?

A: It whaled (wailed).

Q: What kind of house does a pig live in?

A: A hog cabin.

Q: How do frogs send a telegraph?

A: They use Morse toad (code).

Q: How did the frog get over the tall wall?

A: With a tad-pole.

Q: What is a cow's favorite vegetable?

A: Cow-iflower.

Q: Why did the pigs write a lot of letters?

A: Because they were pen pals.

Q: What does a cat wear at night?

A: Its paw-jamas.

Q: What did the night crawler's parents say after their child got home after curfew?

A: "Where on earth have you been?"

"Ode to a Cricket"

Little cricket is up at dawn
Getting dressed, has one shoe on
Little Annie Dachshund came out to play
And she spied Mr. Cricket right away!
Run cricket run
Annie will get you
Cricket ran, cricket flew
Cricket lost his little shoe
Doesn't matter, come what may
Annie got him anyway!

Virginia Satterfield Totsch

Q: Where did the fish go each morning?

A: To their school.

Q: What does a racehorse like to eat for lunch?

A: Fast food.

Q: What do you give a mouse on its birthday?

A: Cheese-cake.

Knock knock!
    Who's there?
Iguana.
    Iguana who?
Iguana come in, so please open up!

Emma: If Noah got milk from the cows, eggs from the chickens, and wool from the sheep on the ark, what did he get from the ducks?

Leah: I don't know, Emma, what?

Emma: Quackers!

Q: Which animal on the ark had the highest IQ?

A: The giraffe!

Q: What do you get when you pour boiling water down a rabbit hole?

A: Hot Cross Bunnies.

Knock knock!
    Who's there?
Owl.
    Owl who?
I'm tired of knocking, so *owl* see you later.

Q: What do cobras put on their bathroom floor?

A: Rep-tiles.

Q: What's a cow's favorite painting?

A: The Moo-na Lisa.

Q: What is a bee's favorite toy?

A: A fris-bee!

Q: What is a dolphin's favorite game show?

A: Whale of Fortune.

Q: What does a goat use when it's camping?

A: A sheeping bag.

Q: What kind of dog is good at chemistry?

A: A Lab-rador retriever.

Q: What is a lightning bug's favorite game?

A: Hide and glow seek.

Q: Why did the cat go to the beauty salon?

A: It needed a pet-icure.

Q: How did the leopard lose its spots?

A: It took a bath and came out spotless.

Q: What did the firefly say before the big race?

A: "Ready, set, glow!"

Did You Know . . .

The tongue of a blue whale can weigh as much as a full-grown elephant.

Q: What did the firefly have for lunch?

A: A light meal.

Q: What did the wolf say when it met its new neighbors?

A: "Howl are you doing?"

Q: Why don't goats mind their own business?

A: Because they're always butting in.

Q: What did the mother possum say to her son?

A: "Quit hanging around all day and do something!"

Q: Why did the cat vanish into thin air?

A: Because it drank evaporated milk.

Q: Where do cows go to dance?

A: The meatball.

Knock knock!
   Who's there?
Seal.
   Seal who?
My lips are sealed until you open the door!

Q: What lives in a hole, has horns, and runs really fast?

A: An ant-elope.

Q: What kind of tree has the most bark?

A: The dogwood tree.

Q: Why didn't the bug feel like doing anything?

A: Because it was a slug.

Q: What's a bird's favorite movie?

A: Batman and Robin.

Q: **What happened to the worm when it didn't clean its room?**

A: It was grounded.

Q: **Why did the cat have trouble using its computer?**

A: Because it kept eating the mouse.

Q: **Why did the mosquito wake up in the middle of the night?**

A: It was having a bite-mare.

Knock knock!
　Who's there?
Goat.
　Goat who?
You're getting my goat—just let me in!

Q: **What is a wolf's favorite treat?**

A: Pigs in a blanket.

Q: **What is a wolf's favorite book?**

A: Little Howl on the Prairie.

Q: **What did the bird wear to the ball?**

A: A duck-sedo (tuxedo).

Q: Why did the dinosaur cross the road?

A: To eat the chickens on the other side.

Q: When can an elephant sit under an umbrella and not get wet?

A: When it's not raining.

Q: What is the sleepiest dinosaur?

A: The Bronto-snore-ous.

Q: What do you get when a rhinoceros goes running through your garden?

A: Squash.

Q: Why did the dog quit playing football?

A: The game got too ruff (rough).

Q: What do you get when you cross a pig and a cow?

A: A ham-burger.

Q: What do you do if a cow won't give milk?

A: You mooove on to the udder one.

Q: Why did the horse wake up in the middle of the night?

A: It was having a night-mare.

Q: What do you get when a pig does karate?

A: Pork chops!

Q: Where do cats shop for their toys?

A: From a toy cat-alog.

Q: How are A's just like flowers?

A: Bees follow them.

Q: Where do fish like to sleep?

A: On their water beds.

Q: What kind of birds like to stick together?

A: Vel-crows.

Q: What do you get when you cross a salmon and an elephant?

A: Swim trunks.

Q: What is a frog's favorite snack?

A: French flies.

Q: What is big, gray, and wears glass slippers?

A: Cinderelephant.

Q: Why do fish make good lawyers?

A: Because they like de-bait.

Q: What do you get when a barn full of cows won't give milk?

A: Udder chaos.

Q: What do you call it when one cow is spying on another cow?

A: A steak out.

Tim: My dog keeps chasing people on a bike!

Tom: Why don't you put him on a leash?

Tim: No, I think I'll just take his bike away.

Q: What's a cow's favorite game?

A: Moo-sical chairs.

Q: What kind of keys never unlock anything?

A: Monkeys, turkeys, and donkeys.

Jill: How do elephants smell?

Jane: Not very good!

Q: What has two heads, four eyes, six legs, and a tail?

A: A cowboy on a horse.

Q: Where do bears keep their clothes?
A: In a claw-set (closet).

Q: What kind of bugs wear sneakers?
A: Shoo flies (shoe flies).

Q: What game do leopards always lose?
A: Hide and seek—they always get spotted.

Q: Why are snails shy at parties?
A: They don't want to come out of their shell.

Q: Why did the bull owe so much money?
A: Because it always charged.

Q: What is a chicken's favorite game?
A: Duck, duck, goose.

Q: Did you hear about the dog that didn't have any teeth?
A: Its bark was worse than its bite.

Q: What do dogs have that no other animals have?
A: Puppies.

Knock knock!
   Who's there?
Fur.
   Fur who?
I'm waiting fur you to open the door!

Q: What has a horn but does not honk?

A: A rhinoceros.

Q: Why do dragons sleep all day?

A: Because they like to hunt knights.

Q: What kind of bone is hard for a dog to eat?

A: A trombone.

Q: How did the gorilla fix its bike?

A: With a monkey wrench.

Q: What is a woodpecker's favorite kind of joke?

A: A knock-knock joke.

Q: What do you call a story about a giraffe?

A: A tall tale.

Q: What did the vet give to the sick parakeet?

A: A special tweetment.

Anna: Can a seagull eat fifty fish in an hour?

Leah: No, but a peli-can!

Q: What kind of bee is good for your health?

A: Vitamin B.

Did you know ...

A platypus is the only mammal that lays eggs.

Q: What do you get when you put a pig in a blender?

A: Bacon bits.

Q: Why do elephants have trunks?

A: Because they would look silly with suitcases.

Q: What kind of dogs can tell time?

A: Watch dogs.

Q: What do you get when you combine a bear and a pig?

A: A teddy boar.

Q: How did the bird open the can of birdseed?

A: With a crow-bar.

Two cockroaches are eating together in a garbage can. One cockroach says to the other, "Did you hear about the new restaurant that opened up down the road? It has the cleanest kitchen I've ever seen. The place sparkles and shines. There isn't a crumb anywhere to be found!" The other cockroach looked up and said, "Please stop! I'm eating here!"

Q: What do woodpeckers eat for breakfast?

A: Oakmeal.

Q: How do dolphins make hard decisions?

A: By flippering a coin.

Q: Why was the lion always tired?

A: It would only take cat naps.

Q: What is the smartest bird in the world?

A: Owl-bert Einstein.

Q: What kind of animal never gets old?

A: A gnu (new).

Q: **How do turkeys travel across the ocean?**

A: In a gravy boat.

Q: **What did the wolf do when he heard the joke?**

A: He howled.

Q: **What did the spider say to the fly?**

A: "Why don't you stick around for a while?"

Q: **How do you grow a blackbird?**

A: Plant some bird seed.

Q: **Why did the turkey have a stomachache?**

A: He gobbled up his food too fast.

Knock knock!
    Who's there?
Bat.
    Bat who?
I bat you're going to let me in soon!

Did You Know . . .

A gnu is another name for a wildebeest.

Q: What did the mouse say when he lost his piece of cheese?

A: Rats!

Q: What is a cat's favorite dessert?

A: Mice cream.

Did You Know . . .

Benjamin Franklin wanted our nation's bird to be a wild turkey instead of the bald eagle.

Q: Where do skunks like to sit in church?

A: In the front pew.

Josh: Should I go see the prairie dogs in Texas?

Anna: Sure Josh, gopher it!

Q: What do you get when you cross a deer and a pirate?

A: A buck-aneer.

Q: Why was the elephant mad at the bellman?

A: He dropped its trunk.

Q: What happened when the giraffes had a race?

A: They were neck and neck the whole time.

Q: Why didn't the llama get any dessert?

A: He wouldn't eat his llama beans (lima beans).

Q: What does a cat do when he wants popcorn in the middle of the movie?

A: He pushes the paws button.

Knock knock!
    Who's there?
Elephant.
    Elephant who?
You forgot to feed the elephant?!

Knock knock!
    Who's there?
Badger.
    Badger who?
I'll stop *badger*ing you if you let me in!

Did You Know . . .

Sloths sleep 80% of the time.

Q: **What do polar bears eat for lunch?**
A: Iceberg-ers.

Q: **How can you tell if a moose has been in your freezer?**
A: By the moose tracks.

Q: **What did one cat say to the other cat?**
A: "Can you hear me meow?"

Knock knock!
    Who's there?
Lion.
    Lion who?
Quit lion around and answer the door already!

Patient: Doctor, I have a problem. I think I'm a moth.

Doctor: I don't think you should be seeing me. I think you need a psychiatrist!

Patient: I know, but I was on my way there and I saw you had your light on.

Patient: Doctor, I think I'm a chicken.

Doctor: How long have you been feeling this way?

Patient: Ever since I was a little egg.

Did You Know . . .

The average hen lays 19 dozen eggs in a year.

Silly Animal Tongue Twisters

(Say these three times as fast as you can!)

Kitty catty, paws, claws, mouse, house, whiskers, tricksters, fur, purr, pounce!

Purple penguins play ping pong.

Bullfrogs blow big bubbles.

Sneaky snakes slither slowly.

Big bears bounce balls.

Skinks think skunks stink.

Beefy blazing bison burgers.

Moths thought sloths got flaws.

3

KNOCK-KNOCK JOKES *for* KIDS

Knock knock.
 Who's there?
Amanda.
 Amanda who?
Amanda fix the plumbing is
 here.

Knock knock.
 Who's there?
Billy Bob Joe Penny.
 Billy Bob Joe Penny who?
Seriously, how many Billy
 Bob Joe Penny's do you
 know?

Knock knock.
 Who's there?
Weirdo.
 Weirdo who?
Weirdo you think you're
 going?

Knock knock.
 Who's there?
Leah.
 Leah who?
Leah the door unlocked
 next time!

Knock knock.
 Who's there?
Alden.
 Alden who?
When you're Alden with
 your dinner, can you
 come out and play?

Knock knock.
 Who's there?
Avery.
 Avery who?
Avery nice person is
 knocking on the door.
 You should come take a
 look.

Knock knock.
Who's there?
Lena.
Lena who?
Lena little closer and I'll tell
you another joke.

Knock knock.
Who's there?
Nick.
Nick who?
You're just in the Nick of
time. I was getting ready
to tell another knock-
knock joke!

Knock knock.
Who's there?
West.
West who?
Let me know if you need a
west from these knock-
knock jokes.

Knock knock.
Who's there?
Leon.
Leon who?
Leon me when you're not
strong.

Knock knock.
Who's there?
Ash.
Ash who?
It sounds like you're
catching a cold.

Knock knock.
Who's there?
Mustache.
Mustache who?
I mustache you a question,
so let me in!

Knock knock.
Who's there?
Jimmy.
Jimmy who?
If you Jimmy a key, I'll let
myself in.

Knock knock.
Who's there?
Will.
Will who?
Will you listen to another
knock-knock joke?

Knock knock.
Who's there?
Erin.
Erin who?
I have to run a quick Erin,
but I'll be back!

Knock knock.
Who's there?
Eddy.
Eddy who?
Eddy-body home?

Knock knock.
Who's there?
Oliver.
Oliver who?
Oliver doors are locked, let
me in!

Knock knock.
Who's there?
Alice.
Alice who?
Well, you know what they
say; Alice fair in love
and war.

Knock knock.
Who's there?
Wendy.
Wendy who?
Wendy wind blows de cradle
will rock.

Knock knock.
Who's there?
Wayne.
Wayne who?
Wayne drops are falling on
my head, can you let me
in?

Knock knock.
Who's there?
Max.
Max who?
Max no difference to me.

Knock knock.
Who's there?
Toby.
Toby who?
Toby or not Toby; that is the question, and you'll have to open up to find out!

Knock knock.
Who's there?
France.
France who?
France stick closer than a brother.

Knock knock.
Who's there?
Peas.
Peas who?
Peas tell me some more knock-knock jokes.

Knock knock.
Who's there?
Gwen.
Gwen who?
Gwen do you think you can come out and play?

Knock knock.
Who's there?
Watson.
Watson who?
Watson the radio?

Knock knock.
Who's there?
Wok.
Wok who?
I wok all the way here, and you won't even let me come in!

Knock knock.
Who's there?
Yeast.
Yeast who?
You could at yeast come to the door and say hi!

Knock knock.
Who's there?
Collie.
Collie who?
Collie-flower is good for you.

140

Knock knock.
Who's there?
Sofa.
Sofa who?
Sofa these have been good knock-knock jokes.

Knock knock
Who's there?
Window.
Window who?
Window I get to hear some more knock-knock jokes?

Knock knock.
Who's there?
Cheese.
Cheese who?
For cheese a jolly good fellow, for cheese a jolly good fellow.

Knock knock.
Who's there?
Boil.
Boil who?
Boil you like this next joke!

Knock knock.
Who's there?
Mushroom.
Mushroom who?
There's mushroom for improvement on that last joke.

Knock knock.
Who's there?
Pizza.
Pizza who?
I'm going to give him a pizza my mind!

Knock knock.
Who's there?
Pesto.
Pesto who?
I hate to make a pesto myself, but I'm going to keep knocking until you open.

Knock knock.
    Who's there?
Gluten.
    Gluten who?
You're going to be a gluten
    for punishment if you
    don't open up!

Knock knock.
    Who's there?
Shellfish.
    Shellfish who?
Don't be shellfish, open up
    and share!

Knock knock.
    Who's there?
Darleen.
    Darleen who?
Please be a Darleen and
    open the door for me.

Knock knock.
    Who's there?
Les.
    Les who?
Les tell some more knock-
    knock jokes!

Knock knock.
    Who's there?
Gino.
    Gino who?
Gino, these knock-knock
    jokes are kind of fun.

Knock knock.
    Who's there?
Gladys.
    Gladys who?
I'm Gladys time for another
    knock-knock joke.

Knock knock.
    Who's there?
Otto.
    Otto who?
You really Otto open the
    door.

Knock knock
    Who's there?
Earl.
    Earl who?
Earl to bed, Earl to rise.

Knock knock.
  Who's there?
Jewel.
  Jewel who?
Jewel have to let me in soon.

Knock knock
  Who's there?
Hobbit.
  Hobbit who?
Sorry, telling knock-knock jokes is a bad hobbit I'm trying to break.

Knock knock.
  Who's there?
Dee.
  Dee who?
Dee cake is in Dee oven.

Knock knock.
  Who's there?
Ben Hur.
  Ben Hur who?
Ben Hur for a while now, can you let me in?

Knock knock.
  Who's there?
Rupert.
  Rupert who?
Rupert your left foot in, Rupert your left foot out.

Knock knock.
  Who's there?
Radio.
  Radio who?
Radio or not, here I come!

Knock knock.
  Who's there?
Allison.
  Allison who?
Allison for someone to come to the door, but I don't hear anybody coming.

Knock knock.
  Who's there?
Sandy.
  Sandy who?
Open up and let's go to the
  Sandy beaches.

Knock knock.
  Who's there?
Penny.
  Penny who?
Penny for your thoughts?

Knock knock.
  Who's there?
Mickey.
  Mickey who?
Mickey won't fit in the
  keyhole, can you let me
  in?

Emma:	Will you remember me in an hour?
Anna:	Yes.
Emma:	Will you remember me in a day?
Anna:	Yes.
Emma:	Will you remember me in a week?
Anna:	Yes.
Emma:	Will you remember me in a month?
Anna:	Yes.
Emma:	Will you remember me in a year?
Anna:	Yes.
Emma:	I don't think you will.
Anna:	Sure I will!
Emma:	Knock knock.
Anna:	Who's there?
Emma:	See, you forgot me already!

Knock knock.
Who's there?
Yule.
Yule who?
Yule never know who it is
unless you open the
door!

Knock knock.
Who's there?
Benjamin.
Benjamin who?
I've Benjamin on my guitar
all day!

Knock knock.
Who's there?
Ear.
Ear who?
Ear is another knock-knock
joke—are you ready?

Knock knock.
Who's there?
Waddle.
Waddle who?
Waddle you do if I tell
another knock-knock
joke?

Knock knock.
Who's there?
Howl.
Howl who?
Howl I open the door if it's
locked?

Knock knock.
Who's there?
Uno.
Uno who?
Uno who this is?

Knock knock.
Who's there?
Scott.
Scott who?
There's Scott to be better a
better knock-knock joke
than this one!

Knock knock.
Who's there?
Wanda.
Wanda who?
Wanda come out and play?

Knock knock.
  Who's there?
Nobel.
  Nobel who?
There was Nobel so I had to
  knock!

Knock knock.
  Who's there?
Mabel.
  Mabel who?
Mabel isn't working right
  either.

Knock knock.
  Who's there?
Leaf.
  Leaf who?
I'm not going to leaf so you
  had better let me in!

Knock knock.
  Who's there?
Figs.
  Figs who?
Figs your doorbell, it's not
  working!

Knock knock.
  Who's there?
Butter.
  Butter who?
Butter open up—it looks
  like rain out here!

Knock knock.
  Who's there?
Udder.
  Udder who?
Would you like to hear an
  udder knock-knock
  joke?

Knock knock.
  Who's there?
Claws.
  Claws who?
Claws the window—it's
  cold in here!

Knock knock.
  Who's there?
Auntie.
  Auntie who?
Auntie going to let me in
  yet?

Knock knock.
Who's there?
Irish.
Irish who?
Irish you would open the
door now!

Knock knock.
Who's there?
Rita.
Rita who?
Rita good book lately?

Knock knock.
Who's there?
Watson.
Watson who?
Can you tell me Watson
your mind?

Knock knock.
Who's there?
Annie.
Annie who?
Annie thing you can do I
can do better.

Knock knock.
Who's there?
Annie.
Annie who?
Annie chance you want to
hear another knock-
knock joke?

Knock knock.
Who's there?
Myth.
Myth who?
I myth seeing you!

Knock knock.
Who's there?
Jacob.
Jacob who?
Jacob your mind! Do you
want to hear another
knock-knock joke?

Knock knock.
Who's there?
Stu.
Stu who?
It's Stu late to ask any
questions!

Knock knock.
    Who's there?
Justin.
    Justin who?
I think I got here Justin
    time!

Knock knock.
    Who's there?
Adolf.
    Adolf who?
Adolf ball hit me on the
    mouth, and my lip
    swelled up.

Knock knock.
    Who's there?
Lionel.
    Lionel who?
Lionel always get you in
    trouble, so tell the truth!

Knock knock.
    Who's there?
Manny.
    Manny who?
How Manny knock-knock
    jokes do you want to
    hear?

Knock knock.
    Who's there?
Dawn.
    Dawn who?
Please Dawn leave me out
    here in the rain.

Knock knock.
    Who's there?
Adore.
    Adore who?
Adore is between you and
    me, so please open up!

Knock knock.
    Who's there?
Eamon.
    Eamon who?
Eamon the mood for some
    more knock-knock
    jokes, how about you?

Knock knock.
    Who's there?
Quiche.
    Quiche who?
Can I have a hug and a
    quiche?

Knock knock.
  Who's there?
Countess.
  Countess who?
**Does this countess a funny
  knock-knock joke?**

Knock knock.
  Who's there?
Kenya.
  Kenya who?
**Kenya open the door,
  please?**

Knock knock.
  Who's there?
Owen.
  Owen who?
**I'm Owen you some money,
  so open up and I'll pay
  you back.**

Knock knock.
  Who's there?
Les.
  Les who?
**Open the door and Les be
  friends!**

Knock knock.
  Who's there?
Norway.
  Norway who?
**There is Norway I'm going
  to just stand here, so
  open the door!**

Knock knock.
  Who's there?
Nacho cheese.
  Nacho cheese who?
**That is nacho cheese, so give
  it back!**

Knock knock.
  Who's there?
You.
  You who?
**You-hoo, it's me, can I come
  in?**

Knock knock.
  Who's there?
Betty.
  Betty who?
**I Betty doesn't know who
  this is!**

Knock knock.
  Who's there?
Robin.
  Robin who?
No, Robin Hood. He steals from the rich and gives to the poor.

Knock knock.
  Who's there?
Misty.
  Misty who?
I misty chance to see you—will you let me come in?

Knock knock.
  Who's there?
Summer.
  Summer who?
Summer these jokes are funny, but some aren't!

Knock knock.
  Who's there?
Sharon.
  Sharon who?
I'm Sharon my cookies if you'll let me in!

Knock knock.
  Who's there?
Hayden.
  Hayden who?
Come out and play Hayden go seek!

Knock knock
  Who's there?
Asaid.
  Asaid who?
Asaid open the door, it's cold out here!

Knock knock.
  Who's there?
Sheri.
  Sheri who?
I'll Sheri my secret if you open the door!

Knock knock.
  Who's there?
Abby.
  Abby who?
Abby stung me on the leg—ouch!

Knock knock.
Who's there?
Abel.
Abel who?
Do you think you're Abel to
let me in now?

Knock knock.
Who's there?
Wallace.
Wallace who?
Wallace fair in love and war!

Knock knock.
Who's there?
Barry.
Barry who?
It's Barry nice to meet you!

Knock knock.
Who's there?
Isaac.
Isaac who?
Isaac of knocking, so please
let me in!

Knock knock.
Who's there?
Judith.
Judith who?
Judith thought these knock-
knock jokes would get
old, but they don't!

Knock knock.
Who's there?
Diane.
Diane who?
I'm Diane to see you, so
open the door!

Knock knock.
Who's there?
Carrie.
Carrie who?
Don't you Carrie that I'm
out here knocking?

Knock knock.
Who's there?
Taryn.
Taryn who?
It's Taryn me up inside that
you won't let me in!

152

Knock knock.
  Who's there?
Annette.
  Annette who?
Annette to use the bathroom, so please open the door!

Knock knock.
  Who's there?
Whale.
  Whale who?
Whale, whale, whale, I see your door is locked again!

Knock knock.
  Who's there?
Art.
  Art who?
Art-2 D-2. May the force be with you!

Knock knock.
  Who's there?
Dexter.
  Dexter who?
Dexter halls with boughs of holly!

Knock knock.
  Who's there?
Hans.
  Hans who?
Hans up—you're under arrest!

Knock knock.
  Who's there?
Delores.
  Delores who?
Delores my shepherd, I shall not want.

Knock knock.
  Who's there?
Isabella.
  Isabella who?
Isabella the door not working?

Knock knock.
  Who's there?
Don.
  Don who?
Don you want to come out and play?

Knock knock.
Who's there?
Woo.
Woo who?
Don't get all excited. It's just a knock-knock joke!

Knock knock.
Who's there?
Ketchup.
Ketchup who?
Let me come in so we can ketchup.

Knock knock.
Who's there?
Lego.
Lego who?
Lego of the doorknob so I can come in!

Knock knock.
Who's there?
Wa.
Wa who?
What are you so excited about?

Knock knock.
Who's there?
Howie.
Howie who?
Do you know Howie doing?

Knock knock.
Who's there?
Train.
Train who?
Someone needs to train you how to open a door.

Knock knock.
Who's there?
Cargo.
Cargo who?
Cargo beep, beep and vroom, vroom!

Knock knock.
Who's there?
Matt.
Matt who?
I'm standing on your welcome Matt, but I don't feel very welcome right now.

Knock knock.
Who's there?
Nicole.
Nicole who?
I'll give you a Nicole if you
let me in.

Knock knock.
Who's there?
Sherwood.
Sherwood who?
Sherwood enjoy coming in
and seeing you!

Knock knock.
Who's there?
Ron.
Ron who?
You can Ron but you can't
hide!

Knock knock.
Who's there?
Andy.
Andy who?
He knocked Andy knocked,
but you won't let him in!

Knock knock.
Who's there?
Stan.
Stan who?
Stan back, I'm coming in!

Knock knock.
Who's there?
Henrietta.
Henrietta who?
Henrietta bug, and now he
has a stomachache.

Knock knock.
Who's there?
Hummus.
Hummus who?
Let me in and I'll hummus
a tune.

Knock knock.
Who's there?
I am.
I am who?
Don't you even know who
you are?

Knock knock.
> Who's there?

Hike.
> Hike who?

I didn't know you liked Japanese poetry. (Haiku)

Knock knock.
> Who's there?

Pumpkin.
> Pumpkin who?

A pumpkin fill up your flat tire.

Knock knock.
> Who's there?

Darren.
> Darren who?

I'm Darren you to tell a funnier knock-knock joke!

Knock knock.
> Who's there?

Evie.
> Evie who?

Evie wonder why I'm knocking at the door?

Knock knock.
> Who's there?

Rufus.
> Rufus who?

Call 911—the Rufus on fire!

Knock knock.
> Who's there?

Wendy.
> Wendy who?

Wendy last time you had your doorbell checked?

Knock knock.
> Who's there?

Funnel.
> Funnel who?

The funnel start once you let me in!

Knock knock.
> Who's there?

I'm.
> I'm who?

Don't you know your own name?

Knock knock.
>Who's there?

Hammond.
>Hammond who?

Let's make some Hammond eggs for breakfast.

Knock knock.
>Who's there?

Butcher.
>Butcher who?

Butcher hand over your heart when you say the pledge of allegiance.

Knock knock.
>Who's there?

Frank.
>Frank who?

Can I be Frank and say I really want you to open the door?

Knock knock.
>Who's there?

Peek-a.
>Peek-a who?

Peek-a-boo!

Knock knock.
>Who's there?

Passion.
>Passion who?

I was just passion through and thought I would say hello.

Knock knock.
>Who's there?

Pasture.
>Pasture who?

It's way pasture bedtime, so you'd better go to sleep!

Knock knock.
>Who's there?

Acid.
>Acid who?

Acid I would stop by, so here I am!

Knock knock.
>Who's there?

Elba.
>Elba who?

Elba happy to tell you another knock-knock joke!

Knock knock.
  Who's there?
Kent.
  Kent who?
I Kent see why you won't
  just open the door.

Knock knock.
  Who's there?
Zany.
  Zany who?
Zany body want to come out
  and play?

Knock knock.
  Who's there?
Brandy.
  Brandy who?
Cowboys Brandy cattle out
  on the ranch.

Knock knock.
  Who's there?
Dots.
  Dots who?
Dots for me to know and
  you to find out.

Knock knock.
  Who's there?
Frasier.
  Frasier who?
I'm a Frasier going to have
  to let me in eventually.

Knock knock.
  Who's there?
Woody.
  Woody who?
Woody like to hear another
  knock-knock joke?

Knock knock.
  Who's there?
Freeze.
  Freeze who?
Freeze a jolly good fellow,
  freeze a jolly good
  fellow.

Knock knock.
  Who's there?
Roy.
  Roy who?
Roy, Roy, Roy your boat
  gently down the stream.

Knock knock.
　　Who's there?
Wallaby.
　　Wallaby who?
Wallaby a monkey's uncle!

Knock knock.
　　Who's there?
Ivan.
　　Ivan who?
Ivan idea—let's tell more knock-knock jokes!

Knock knock.
　　Who's there?
Vera.
　　Vera who?
Is Vera way you could open the door?

Knock knock.
　　Who's there?
Snow.
　　Snow who?
Snow use—I'll never run out of knock-knock jokes!

Knock knock.
　　Who's there?
Bond.
　　Bond who?
You're bond to succeed if you try, try again.

Knock knock.
　　Who's there?
Bruce.
　　Bruce who?
I'll Bruce my knuckles if I keep on knocking!

Knock knock.
　　Who's there?
Elsie.
　　Elsie who?
Elsie you later!

Knock knock.
　　Who's there?
Luca.
　　Luca who?
Luca through the keyhole and you'll see who it is!

Knock knock.
>Who's there?

Waddle.
>Waddle who?

**Waddle you give me if I stop
knocking and go away?**

Knock knock.
>Who's there?

Wade.
>Wade who?

**Wade a minute—I want to
tell you another knock-
knock joke!**

Knock knock.
>Who's there?

Megan.
>Megan who?

**It's Megan me mad that you
won't open the door!**

Knock knock.
>Who's there?

Ethan.
>Ethan who?

**Ethan if you don't open the
door, I'll still like you.**

Knock knock.
>Who's there?

Ima.
>Ima who?

**Ima waiting to hear another
knock-knock joke!**

Knock knock.
>Who's there?

Marilee.
>Marilee who?

**Marilee, Marilee, Marilee,
Marilee, life is but a
dream!**

Knock knock.
>Who's there?

Sorry.
>Sorry who?

**Sorry, I think I'm knocking
on the wrong door.**

Knock knock.
>Who's there?

Aaron.
>Aaron who?

**The Aaron here is kind of
stuffy.**

Knock knock.
    Who's there?
Ben.
    Ben who?
**Ben away for a while, but
    I'm back now.**

Knock knock.
    Who's there?
Cantaloupe.
    Cantaloupe who?
**You cantaloupe—you're too
    young to get married!**

Knock knock.
    Who's there?
Stan.
    Stan who?
**I can't Stan it anymore,
    tell me another knock-
    knock joke.**

Knock knock.
    Who's there?
Taylor.
    Taylor who?
**Taylor another knock-knock
    joke!**

Knock knock.
    Who's there?
Kay.
    Kay who?
**Is it O-Kay if I tell another
    knock-knock joke?**

Knock knock.
    Who's there?
Ice cream soda.
    Ice cream soda who?
**Ice cream soda people can
    hear me!**

Knock knock.
    Who's there?
Yugo.
    Yugo who?
**Yugo first, and I'll go
    second.**

Knock knock.
    Who's there?
Vanessa.
    Vanessa who?
**Vanessa door going to open
    up?**

Knock knock.
　Who's there?
Wilma.
　Wilma who?
Wilma breakfast be ready
　pretty soon?

Knock knock.
　Who's there?
Macon.
　Macon who?
I'm Macon my own key to
　open this door!

Knock knock.
　Who's there?
Rudy.
　Rudy who?
It's Rudy never says please
　or thank you.

Knock knock.
　Who's there?
Bonnie.
　Bonnie who?
My Bonnie lies over the
　ocean.

Knock knock.
　Who's there?
Theodore.
　Theodore who?
Theodore is locked, so
　please let me in!

Knock knock.
　Who's there?
Anita.
　Anita who?
Anita hear another knock-
　knock joke!

Knock knock.
　Who's there?
Olive.
　Olive who?
Since Olive here, I think you
　should let me in!

Knock knock.
　Who's there?
Sadie.
　Sadie who?
If I Sadie magic word
　will you let me in . . .
　P-L-E-A-S-E?

Knock knock.
  Who's there?
Michael.
  Michael who?
I Michael you on the phone if you don't answer the door!

Knock knock.
  Who's there?
Bill.
  Bill who?
I'll pay the Bill for dinner if you open the door!

Knock knock.
  Who's there?
Francis.
  Francis who?
Francis in Europe, and Brazil is in South America.

Knock knock.
  Who's there?
Tokyo.
  Tokyo who?
What Tokyo so long to open the door?

Knock knock.
  Who's there?
Olive.
  Olive who?
Olive you!

Knock knock.
  Who's there?
Colin.
  Colin who?
From now on I'm Colin you on the phone!

Knock knock.
  Who's there?
Sarah.
  Sarah who?
Sarah reason you're not opening the door?

Knock knock.
  Who's there?
Donut.
  Donut who?
Donut make you laugh when people tell knock-knock jokes?

Knock knock.
> Who's there?

Mummy.
> Mummy who?

Mummy said you can come
out and play.

Knock knock.
> Who's there?

Muffin.
> Muffin who?

Muffin much going on
around here.

Knock knock.
> Who's there?

Coke.
> Coke who?

Are you calling me crazy?

Knock knock.
> Who's there?

Waffle.
> Waffle who?

It's waffle that you still
haven't opened the
door!

Knock knock.
> Who's there?

Fannie.
> Fannie who?

If Fannie body calls, tell
them I went to the store.

Knock knock.
> Who's there?

Kanga.
> Kanga who?

No, kangaroo.

Knock knock.
> Who's there?

Noah.
> Noah who?

Noah don't think I'll tell you
another knock-knock
joke!

Knock knock.
> Who's there?

Leaf.
> Leaf who?

Leaf me alone so I can read
my joke book!

Knock knock.
    Who's there?
Della.
    Della who?
Open the door so I can
    Della another knock-
    knock joke.

Knock knock.
    Who's there?
Reed.
    Reed who?
Reed a good book lately?

Knock knock.
    Who's there?
Walt.
    Walt who?
Walt! Who goes there?

Knock knock.
    Who's there?
Philip.
    Philip who?
Philip your water bottle if
    you're thirsty.

Knock knock.
    Who's there?
Hawaii.
    Hawaii who?
I'm doing fine, thanks.
    Hawaii doing?

Knock knock.
    Who's there?
Fanny.
    Fanny who?
Fanny you should ask!

Knock knock.
    Who's there?
Lorraine.
    Lorraine who?
Lorraine is coming down, so
    give me an umbrella!

Knock knock.
    Who's there?
Randy.
    Randy who?
I Randy whole way here, so
    open up!

Knock knock.
Who's there?
Reggie.
Reggie who?
Reggie to open the door
yet?

Knock knock.
Who's there?
Rich.
Rich who?
Rich knock-knock joke is
your favorite?

Knock knock.
Who's there?
Dwight.
Dwight who?
Dwight key will get the door
open.

Knock knock.
Who's there?
Chad.
Chad who?
Chad don't you recognize
me? I'm your son!

Knock knock.
Who's there?
Landon.
Landon who?
Is it true cats always Landon
their feet?

Knock knock.
Who's there?
Les.
Les who?
Les you think I'm a stranger,
look through the
keyhole and you will
see.

Knock knock.
Who's there?
Meg.
Meg who?
Meg up your mind—are
you going to let me in or
aren't you?

Knock knock.
Who's there
Doris.
Doris who?
If the Doris locked, I can't come in.

Knock knock.
Who's there?
New Hampshire.
New Hampshire who?
New Hampshire you're not going to open the door.

Knock knock.
Who's there?
Macon.
Macon who?
You're Macon me mad with all this knocking I'm having to do!

Knock knock.
Who's there?
Yukon.
Yukon who?
It's okay, Yukon tell me!

Knock knock.
Who's there?
Watson.
Watson who?
Watson TV tonight?

Knock knock.
Who's there?
Pig.
Pig who?
I'm going to pig the lock if you don't open the door and let me in!

Knock knock.
Who's there?
Juno.
Juno who?
Juno who this is, so open up already!

Knock knock.
Who's there?
Albert.
Albert who?
Do Alberts fly south for the winter?

Knock knock.
> Who's there?

Alvin.
> Alvin who?

We're Alvin a great time out
here!

Knock knock.
> Who's there?

Figs.
> Figs who?

Figs your phone so I can
give you a call!

Knock knock.
> Who's there?

Alma.
> Alma who?

Alma knock-knock jokes are
really funny!

Knock knock.
> Who's there?

Alex.
> Alex who?

Alex the questions around
here!

Knock knock.
> Who's there?

Sherwood.
> Sherwood who?

Sherwood be nice if you'd
open the door.

Knock knock.
> Who's there?

Abbott.
> Abbott who?

Abbott time you asked!

Knock knock.
> Who's there?

Abel.
> Abel who?

Abel rings every time an
angel gets its wings.

Knock knock.
> Who's there?

Annette.
> Annette who?

Annette another glass of
water, open up!

Knock knock.
    Who's there?
To.
    To who?
To whom!

Knock knock.
    Who's there?
Pizza.
    Pizza who?
Pizza really nice guy.

Knock knock.
    Who's there?
Mickey.
    Mickey who?
Mickey won't unlock this door, so please let me in!

Knock knock.
    Who's there?
Cash.
    Cash who?
No thanks, I'd rather have some peanuts.

Knock knock.
    Who's there?
Luke.
    Luke who?
Luke through the window and you'll see who's knocking.

Knock knock.
    Who's there?
Roach.
    Roach who?
I roach you a letter, but I wanted to deliver it in person.

Knock knock.
    Who's there?
Abby.
    Abby who?
Abby birthday to you, Abby birthday to you!

Knock knock.
  Who's there?
Alberta.
  Alberta who?
**Alberta can't guess in a
  million years!**

Knock knock.
  Who's there?
Anna.
  Anna who?
**Anna one, Anna two, Anna
  three!**

Knock knock.
  Who's there?
Dozen.
  Dozen who?
**Dozen anyone ever open
  their door anymore?**

Knock knock.
  Who's there?
Hair.
  Hair who?
**Hair today and gone
  tomorrow.**

Knock knock.
  Who's there?
Ken.
  Ken who?
Ken you hear me now?

Knock knock.
  Who's there?
Alpaca.
  Alpaca who?
**Alpaca suitcase for our
  vacation.**

Knock knock.
  Who's there?
Dishes.
  Dishes who?
Dishes me, open up!

Knock knock.
  Who's there?
Candice.
  Candice who?
Candice joke get any worse?

Knock knock.
> Who's there?

Tibet.
> Tibet who?

Early Tibet, early to rise.

Knock knock.
> Who's there?

Tank.
> Tank who?

You're welcome!

Knock knock.
> Who's there?

Andy.
> Andy who?

Andy shoots, Andy scores!

Knock knock.
> Who's there?

Owls.
> Owls who?

Why yes, they do!

Knock knock.
> Who's there?

Otter.
> Otter who?

You otter open the door and
> let me in!

Knock knock.
> Who's there?

Bacon.
> Bacon who?

I'm bacon some cookies. Do
> you want one?

Knock knock.
> Who's there?

Haven.
> Haven who?

Haven you heard enough
> of these knock-knock
> jokes?

Knock knock.
> Who's there?

Anita.
> Anita who?

Anita drink of water, so
> please let me in!

Josh:	**Knock knock.**
Leah:	Who's there?
Josh:	**Banana.**
Leah:	Banana who?
Josh:	**Knock knock.**
Leah:	Who's there?
Josh:	**Banana.**
Leah:	Banana who?
Josh:	**Knock knock.**
Leah:	Who's there?
Josh:	**Banana.**
Leah:	Banana who?
Josh:	**Knock knock.**
Leah:	Who's there?
Josh:	**Orange.**
Leah:	Orange who?
Josh:	**Orange you glad this joke is over?**

Knock knock.
Who's there?
Pitcher.
Pitcher who?
**Bless you! Are you catching
a cold?**

Knock knock.
Who's there?
Alex.
Alex who?
**Alex-plain when you open
the door!**

Knock knock.
Who's there?
Elsie.
Elsie who?
Elsie you later!

Knock knock.
Who's there?
Ears.
Ears who?
Ears looking at you, kid.

Knock knock.
Who's there?
Lydia.
Lydia who?
**The Lydia fell off and made
a big mess out here;
please open up.**

Knock knock.
Who's there?
Nun.
Nun who?
Nun of your business.

Knock knock.
Who's there?
June.
June who?
**June know how long I've
been knocking out here?**

Knock knock.
Who's there?
August.
August who?
**August of wind almost blew
me away!**

Knock knock.
    Who's there?
Spell.
    Spell who?
W-H-O.

Knock knock.
    Who's there?
Police.
    Police who?
**Police come out and play
    with me!**

Knock knock.
    Who's there?
Jamaica.
    Jamaica who?
**Jamaica good sandwich? I'm
    hungry!**

Knock knock.
    Who's there?
Ally.
    Ally who?
**Ally really want to do is tell
    another knock-knock
    joke!**

Knock knock.
    Who's there?
Eve.
    Eve who?
**I'll Eve you alone if you
    want me to.**

Knock knock.
    Who's there?
Whale.
    Whale who?
**I'll start to whale if you
    don't let me in.**

Knock knock.
    Who's there?
Ima.
    Ima who?
**Ima really glad to see you
    today!**

Knock knock.
    Who's there?
Jonah.
    Jonah who?
**Jonah anybody who will
    open the door for me?**

Knock knock.
Who's there?
Cain.
Cain who?
Cain you open the door for me, it's very cold out here!

Knock knock.
Who's there?
Dishes.
Dishes who?
Dishes a really dumb knock-knock joke!

Knock knock.
Who's there?
Ada.
Ada who?
Ada lot of sweets, and now I feel sick!

Knock knock.
Who's there?
Adam.
Adam who?
Adam all up and see how much you have!

Knock knock.
Who's there?
Jell-o.
Jell-o who?
Jell-o, it's me again!

Knock knock.
Who's there?
Barbie.
Barbie who?
Barbie-Q.

Knock knock.
Who's there?
Peas.
Peas who?
Peas come outside and play with me!

Knock knock.
Who's there?
Fanny.
Fanny who?
If Fanny body asks, tell them I'm not home.

Knock knock.
Who's there?
Jess.
Jess who?
Jess me and my shadow.

Knock knock.
Who's there?
Baby oil.
Baby oil who?
Baby oil will, and baby oil won't!

Knock knock.
Who's there?
Canoe.
Canoe who?
Canoe come out and play?

Knock knock.
Who's there?
Oldest.
Oldest who?
Oldest knocking is giving me a headache.

Knock knock.
Who's there?
Woody.
Woody who?
Woody like to hear another knock-knock joke?

Knock knock.
Who's there?
Weed.
Weed who?
Weed better go home—it's time for dinner!

Knock knock.
Who's there?
Juan.
Juan who?
I Juan to tell you another knock-knock joke.

Knock knock.
Who's there?
Anita.
Anita who?
Anita minute to think of another knock-knock joke.

Knock knock.
> Who's there?

Amos.
> Amos who?

Amos-quito bit me on the arm!

Knock knock.
> Who's there?

Andy.
> Andy who?

Andy bit me again.

Knock knock.
> Who's there?

Colin.
> Colin who?

I'll be Colin you later.

Knock knock.
> Who's there?

Rockefeller.
> Rockefeller who?

You can Rockefeller to sleep in his cradle.

Knock knock
> Who's there?

Water.
> Water who?

Water your favorite knock-knock jokes?

Knock knock.
> Who's there?

Conner.
> Conner who?

Conner tell me another joke that's as funny as the last one?

Knock knock.
> Who's there?

Dragon.
> Dragon who?

Quit dragon your feet and open the door!

Knock knock.
> Who's there?

Ringo.
> Ringo who?

Ringo round the rosie!

Knock knock.
  Who's there?
Willie.
  Willie who?
**Willie ever open the door
  and let me in?**

Knock knock.
  Who's there?
Wanda.
  Wanda who?
**I Wanda where I put my car
  keys.**

Knock knock.
  Who's there?
Moe.
  Moe who?
**Moe knock-knock jokes,
  please!**

Knock knock.
  Who's there?
Ernest.
  Ernest who?
Ernest is full of eggs!

Knock knock.
  Who's there?
Taylor.
  Taylor who?
**Taylor brother to pick up
  his toys.**

Knock knock.
  Who's there?
Dewy.
  Dewy who?
**Dewy have a key to open
  this door, or do I have
  to go through the
  window?**

Knock knock.
  Who's there?
Lettuce.
  Lettuce who?
**Lettuce know when you can
  come out and play!**

Knock knock.
Who's there?
Nose.
Nose who?
Nose anymore good knock-knock jokes?

Knock knock.
Who's there?
Watt.
Watt who?
Watt, you want to hear another knock-knock joke?

Knock knock.
Who's there?
Juicy.
Juicy who?
Juicy any monsters under my bed?

Knock knock.
Who's there?
Yellow.
Yellow who?
Yellow, how are you doing today?

Knock knock.
Who's there?
Raymond.
Raymond who?
Raymond me to buy milk at the store.

Knock knock.
Who's there?
Doughnut.
Doughnut who?
Doughnut open the door to strangers!

Knock knock.
Who's there?
Handsome.
Handsome who?
Handsome snacks over here—I'm really hungry!

Knock knock.
Who's there?
Rabbit.
Rabbit who?
Rabbit carefully—it's a special present!

Knock knock.
Who's there?
Sarah.
Sarah who?
Is Sarah a doctor in the
house?

Knock knock.
Who's there?
Oscar.
Oscar who?
Oscar silly question and get
a silly answer!

Knock knock.
Who's there?
Who.
Who who?
What, are you an owl or
something?

Knock knock.
Who's there?
Gorilla.
Gorilla who?
Gorilla me a hamburger, I'm
hungry!

Knock knock.
Who's there?
Conrad.
Conrad who?
Conrad-ulations! That was a
great knock-knock joke!

Knock knock.
Who's there?
Walter.
Walter who?
Walter you doing here so
early?

Knock knock.
Who's there?
Everest.
Everest who?
Everest, or is it work, work,
work?

Knock knock.
Who's there?
Lion.
Lion who?
Quit lion around and open
the door!

Knock knock.
   Who's there?
Thatcher.
   Thatcher who?
Thatcher was a good knock-
   knock joke. Can you tell
   another one?

Knock knock.
   Who's there?
Peace.
   Peace who?
Peace porridge hot, peace
   porridge cold.

4

MORE LAUGH -OUT- LOUD JOKES

for

KIDS

Knock knock.

Who's there?

Chew.

Chew who?

I want to hang out with chew so let me in!

Mark: **What's the best place to chop down a Christmas tree?**

Tim: I'm not sure.

Mark: **About three inches off the ground.**

Q: Why did the broccoli slap the lettuce?

A: Because it was being fresh!

Q: Why did the elephants take up the least amount of room on Noah's ark?

A: Because they kept everything in their trunks!

Q: Why did the moon feel sick to its stomach?

A: It was a full moon.

Suzy: I'm so smart I can sing the whole alphabet song!

Jimmy: That's nothing. I can sing it in lower case and capitals!

Q: Why were the lamb and goat such good friends?

A: Because they had a very close relation-sheep.

Q: What do you get when you spill your coffee in the dirt?

A: Coffee grounds!

Q: What kind of vegetable has the worst manners?

A: A rude-abaga.

Q: What is penguin's favorite kind of food?

A: Ice-burgers.

Q: What do you get when you brush your teeth with dish soap?

A: Bubble gums.

Q: What kind of trees wear mittens?

A: Palm trees.

Q: Why was the library so busy?

A: It was overbooked.

Q: **What do you get when you cross a porcupine with a snail?**

A: A slowpoke.

Q: **When do farmers go bald?**

A: When they have re-seeding hairlines.

Q: **How do you know when it's been raining cats and dogs?**

A: When you step in a poodle.

> **Justin:** **Do you know how to make a pineapple shake?**
>
> **Nate:** You mix pineapple, milk, and ice cream?
>
> **Justin:** **No, you take it to a scary movie!**

Q: **What do you get when you cross an owl and bubble gum?**

A: A bird that will chews wisely.

Knock knock.

> Who's there?

Leon.

> Leon who?

I'd be Leon if I told you I didn't love knock-knock jokes!

Q: What kind of homework do you do on the couch?

A: Multipli-cushion.

Tim: Did you hear about the guy who stuck his finger in a light socket?

Scott: No, what happened?

Tim: It was shocking!

Q: How does a cow get to the office?

A: On a cow-moo-ter train.

Q: What do you get when you cross a dinosaur and gunpowder?

A: Dino-mite.

Q: Why shouldn't you stare at the turkey dressing at Thanksgiving?

A: The turkey will be embarrassed.

Q: Why did the skeleton refuse to go to the dance?

A: He had no-body to dance with.

Q: Why did the suspenders have to go to jail?

A: They held up a pair of pants.

Q: Why don't fish ever get a summer vacation?

A: They spend every day in schools.

Q: What do you get when you play tug-of-war with a pig?

A: Pulled pork.

> **Joe:** Can you believe that I ate six helpings of spaghetti last night?
>
> **Bill:** Well, I wouldn't put it pasta!

Q: Why did the orange have to stop and take a nap?

A: It ran out of juice.

Q: What do you call a boomerang that won't come back to you?

A: A stick.

Q: Did you hear about the new restaurant they put on Mars?

A: I hear the food is out of this world.

Q: How much did Santa pay for his reindeer?

A: Just a few bucks. They didn't cost him much doe.

Q: What is a trumpet player's favorite month of the year?

A: March.

Sally: What is a mummy's favorite kind of music?

Bill: I'm not sure.

Sally: Wrap music!

Q: Why couldn't the fish go shopping?

A: It didn't have anemone.

Andrew: Do you know how to spell "hard water" using only three letters?

Dave: I'm pretty sure that's impossible!

Andrew: No, it isn't. I-C-E is hard water!

Q: What kind of motorcycle do bulls like to ride?

A: They ride a Cow-asaki.

Q: What does a grizzly do on a hard day?

A: He'll just grin and bear it.

Q: How many months have 28 days?

A: All twelve of them do!

Knock knock.

Who's there?

Bean.

Bean who?

Its bean way too long since you've heard a knock-knock joke!

Q: What do you call a pumpkin that watches over you?
A: A body-gourd.

Q: What do you call a greasy bug?
A: A butter-fly.

Q: Why did the whale cross the ocean?
A: To get to the other tide.

Q: Why did the rabbit need to relax?
A: He was feeling jumpy.

Q: Why did the skunk cross the road?
A: To get to the odor side!

Q: What do you get when you combine an elephant and a skunk?
A: A smell-ephant.

Q: What kind of vegetable is hip and cool?

A: A radish.

Q: How do you sneak across the desert without being seen?

A: You wear camel-flage.

Q: What is a maple's favorite class at school?

A: Geometree.

Knock knock.

Who's there?

Arthur.

Arthur who?

Arthur any more funny knock-knock jokes?

Q: Why wouldn't the turkey eat any pumpkin pie?

A: It was too stuffed.

Q: What do you call bears with no ears?

A: B!

Q: What happened when the turkey got in a fight?

A: He got the stuffing knocked out of him.

Knock knock.

Who's there?

Annie.

Annie who?

Annie chance I could tell you another knock-knock joke?

Q: What does a black belt eat for lunch?
A: Kung food!

Q: Why did the lobster get grounded by his parents?
A: He was always getting himself in hot water!

Q: What kind of automobile is the same going backward and forward?
A: Racecar.

Knock knock.

Who's there?

Gus.

Gus who?

I bet you can't Gus who this is!

Q: What did the skunks do on Saturday night?

A: They watched a movie on their smell-evision.

Q: What do you call bunny's prized possessions?

A: Hare-looms.

Q: What do you get when you combine a kitty and a fish?

A: A purr-anha!

Q: What do fish like to sing during the holidays?

A: Christmas corals.

Q: What do you get when you drop a pumpkin from your roof?

A: Squash.

Q: Why did the apples want to hang out with the banana?

A: Because it was so appeeling.

Q: Why couldn't the skeletons play any music?

A: They didn't have any organs.

Adel: My math book fell into my jack-o'-lantern the other day.

Anna: What did you do?

Adel: I made pumpkin pi.

Q: What did the blackbird use to get the door open?
A: A crow bar!

Q: What do you call kids who play outside in the snow?
A: Chilled-ren.

Q: What did the almond say to the psychiatrist?
A: "Everybody says I'm nuts!"

Q: Why was the skeleton laughing?
A: Somebody tickled its funny bone.

Q: How do you keep a restaurant safe from criminals?
A: Use a burger alarm.

Q: What does a cat eat for breakfast?
A: Mice Krispies.

Q: How does a pig get to the hospital?
A: In a ham-bulance.

Q: What do you get when you cross a dog and broccoli?

A: Collie-flower.

Q: What language do pigs speak?

A: French, because they go "Oui, oui, oui," all the way home!

Q: What has a head and a tail, but no body?

A: A penny.

Q: What do you feed a teddy bear?

A: Stuffing!

Q: Why did the elf get in trouble with his teacher?

A: He didn't do his gnomework.

Q: What do you get when you cross a snake with dessert?

A: A pie-thon.

> **Dave:** What do you get when you cross an airplane, a car, and a cat?
>
> **Bill:** I give up.
>
> **Dave:** A flying car-pet!

Q: What kind of homework do you do in a taxi?

A: Vocabulary.

Q: What has a face and two hands, but no arms or legs?

A: A clock!

Q: How do you make friends with everyone at school?

A: Become the princi-pal.

Q: What do you get when you play basketball in Hawaii?

A: Hula-Hoops!

Q: What is a snowman's favorite cereal?

A: Frosted Flakes.

Q: What do you call a boy with no money in his pocket?

A: Nickel-less.

Q: How did the oyster get to the doctor?

A: In a clam-bulance.

Q: Why was the snake so funny?

A: His jokes were hiss-terical.

Knock knock.

Who's there?

Whale.

Whale who?

Whale you let me tell you another knock-knock joke?

Q: What is a sailor's favorite kind of book to read?
A: Ferry tales.

Q: Which word in the dictionary is always spelled wrong?
A: WRONG, of course!

Q: What does a monster put on top of his hot fudge sundae?
A: Whipped scream.

Q: Why did the burglar steal the eggs?
A: He likes his eggs poached!

Q: Why can't you ever trust an atom?
A: They make up everything!

Q: Why did the chef have to stop cooking?
A: He ran out of thyme.

Q: What is an elephant's favorite vegetable?

A: Squash.

Q: How do frogs get the ice off their car windows?

A: They use the defrogger.

Q: How do you know if you have an elephant in your refrigerator?

A: The refrigerator door won't shut!

Q: What did the tornado say to the race car?

A: "Can I take you for a spin?"

Q: What does a weasel like to read?

A: Pop-up books!

Q: What is a squirrel's favorite ballet?

A: The Nutcracker!

Q: How did everyone know that the lion swallowed the bear?

A: His stomach was growling.

Q: What do frogs like with their cheeseburgers?

A: French flies and a croak.

Q: What is the best thing to do with a blue whale?

A: Tell it a joke and cheer it up!

Q: What happened to the dog after it swallowed the watch?

A: It was full of ticks.

Q: What kind of shoes do foxes wear?

A: Sneak-ers.

Q: What did the baker say when his cookie wouldn't crumble?

A: "That's one tough cookie!"

Q: What did the bee say to the flower?

A: "Hi, honey!"

Q: What did the flower say to the bee?

A: "Buzz off!"

Q: What did the picture say when the police showed up?

A: "I didn't do it—I've been framed!"

Q: Why did the king go to the dentist?

A: Because he wanted a crown on his tooth!

Q: Why was the comedian sad?

A: He thought his life was a joke!

Knock knock.

Who's there?

Auto.

Auto who?

You really auto tell me some knock-knock jokes!

Q: Why did the book join the police force?

A: It wanted to go undercover!

Q: What do you get when you cross a bird and a bee?

A: A buzzard.

Q: Why did the elephant quit his job?

A: He was working for peanuts.

Q: What do you get when you throw a couch in the pond?

A: A sitting duck!

Q: What do you get when you cross a horse and a pencil?

A: Horseback writing.

Q: Why did the policeman go to the baseball game?

A: He heard someone had stolen second base.

Q: What kinds of keys are easy to swallow?

A: Cookies.

Knock knock.

Who's there?

Ken.

Ken who?

Ken I tell you another knock-knock joke?

Q: Why did the horse go to the psychiatrist?

A: It was feeling un-stable.

Q: What kind of sea creatures are the most musical?

A: Fish, because they have so many scales!

Q: When do you know a tiger isn't telling the truth?

A: When it's a lion.

Q: Why did the baker go to work every day?

A: He really kneaded the dough!

Q: What did the bumblebee say to his wife?

A: "Honey, you're bee-utiful."

Q: Where does a cow go when it's hungry?

A: To the calf-eteria.

Knock knock.

Who's there?

Tibet.

Tibet who?

Early Tibet, early to rise.

Bob: Did you hear about the farmer who wrote a joke book?

Bill: No, is it any good?

Bob: The jokes are really corn-y.

Q: What does a moose like to play at parties?

A: Moose-ical chairs.

Q: Who leads the orchestra at the zoo?

A: The boa-conductor.

Q: What did the drum say to the violin?

A: "Stop harping at me!"

Q: What do little cows give?

A: Condensed milk.

Q: What does a possum like to do for fun?

A: Hang out with its friends!

Q: Who helped the mermaid go to the ball?

A: Her fairy cod-mother.

Knock knock.

Who's there?

Hector.

Hector who?

When the Hector you going to open the door?

Q: What does a snowman eat for dessert?

A: Ice krispy treats.

Emma: Can February March?

Leah: No, but April May.

Q: What do you call someone with no body and no nose?

A: No-body knows.

Q: Which has more courage, a rock or a tree?

A: A rock—it's boulder!

Q: Why did the plant go to the dentist?

A: It needed a root canal!

Josh: Do you think change is hard?

Joe: I sure do—have you ever tried to bend a quarter?

Patient: Hey doc, I think I broke my leg in two places. What should I do?

Doctor: Don't go to those two places anymore!

Knock knock.

Who's there?

Minnow.

Minnow who?

If you can think of a better knock-knock joke, let minnow.

John: I'm really bright.

Jane: How bright are you?

John: I'm so bright, my mother calls me sun.

Jill: I'm upset that my new toaster isn't waterproof.

Jen: What's so bad about that?

Jill: When I found out, I was shocked!

Q: How do fleas travel from one dog to another?

A: They itchhike their way there!

Q: What is a swan's favorite Christmas carol?

A: Duck the Halls.

Q: Why did the chicken go to bed?

A: It was eggs-hausted.

Knock knock.

Who's there?

Gas.

Gas who?

I bet you can't gas who this is at the door!

Q: What is something that has to be broken before you can use it?

A: An egg!

Knock knock.

Who's there?

Window.

Window who?

Window you want to hear another great knock-knock joke?

Bill: Do you know who told me you sound like an owl when you talk?

Joe: No, who?

Q: What did the fork say to the butter knife?

A: "You're so dull."

Q: What do you get from an invisible cow?

A: Evaporated milk.

Q: What do you get when you cross a dentist and a boat?

A: A tooth ferry.

Q: **Why did the boy eat his homework?**

A: The teacher said it would be a piece of cake.

Q: **Why did the banana put on sunscreen?**

A: It didn't want to peel.

Q: **Why did the Starburst go to school?**

A: It wanted to be a Smartie.

Patient: **Doc, I think I'm turning into a piano.**

Doc: Well, that's just grand!

Q: **Where do you learn to cut wood?**

A: At boarding school.

Q: **Where does a volcano wash its hands?**

A: In the lava-tory.

Q: **Why did the wheel stop turning?**

A: It was too tired.

Q: **What goes up but doesn't come back down?**

A: Your age!

Q: How did the pig write a letter?

A: With a pig pen.

Q: Which giraffe won the race?

A: It was a tie—they were neck and neck the whole time.

Q: What does a pig use when it has a rash?

A: Oinkment.

Q: Why did the tree need to take a nap?

A: It was bushed.

Knock knock.

Who's there?

Pecan.

Pecan who?

You should pecan someone your own size!

Q: What has four wheels and flies?

A: A garbage truck!

Q: What is the worst day of the week for fish?

A: Fryday!

Q: What kind of buttons does everyone wear?

A: Belly buttons.

Q: How do you repair a squashed tomato?

A: Use tomato paste!

Q: What is a soda's favorite subject in school?

A: Fizzics.

Q: What sometimes runs but never walks?

A: Your nose!

Q: What is a cow's favorite painting?

A: The Moona Lisa.

Knock knock.

Who's there?

Rita.

Rita who?

Did you Rita good book lately?

Knock knock.

Who's there?

Ears.

Ears who?

Ears looking at you, kid.

Q: What is the best time to see the dentist?

A: At tooth-thirty.

Q: What kind of tree needs a doctor all the time?

A: A sycamore tree.

Q: Why did the bathtub need a vacation?

A: Because it was drained.

Q: What kind of vegetable is lazy and irresponsible?

A: A dead-beet.

Q: Why did the meteorite go to Hollywood?

A: It wanted to be a star.

Q: What do you get when you cross a snowman and a lion?

A: Frost-bite.

Q: What do you get when you throw noodles in a Jacuzzi?

A: Spa-ghetti.

Q: When is a cow happy, then sad, and then angry?

A: When it's moo-dy.

Q: What did the ocean say to the fishing boat?

A: Nothing—it just waved.

Q: Which of Santa's reindeer has the worst manners?

A: Rude-olph.

Q: Why did the inventor get struck by lightning?

A: He was brain-storming.

Q: What did the one maple leaf say to the other maple leaf?

A: "I'm falling for you!"

Q: Why did the stereo explode?

A: It was radio-active.

Q: How do you know when a bucket is feeling sick?

A: When it looks a little pail.

Q: What plays music on your head?

A: A head-band.

Q: What kind of bird do you have with every meal?

A: A swallow.

Q: What do you call a lion that gives you presents?

A: Santa Claws.

Q: What do you get when you cross a flower, a car, and the USA?

A: A pink car nation.

Q: What did Mrs. Claus say to Santa when he was complaining about the rain on Christmas Eve?

A: "Oh, let it rain, dear."

Q: What's a hyena's favorite kind of cookie?

A: A snickerdoodle.

Q: Why can't a beaver use a computer?

A: It doesn't know how to log in.

Q: What do you call your dog when it goes deaf?

A: It doesn't matter—it can't hear you anyway!

Q: How much did Santa's sleigh cost?

A: Nothing—it was on the house!

Q: What is a skeleton's favorite instrument?

A: A trombone.

Q: Why didn't the panda bear get the job?

A: It didn't have the right koala-fications.

> **Sally:** Can you believe I gave my pigs a bath?
> **Susie:** That's a bunch of hog wash!

Q: Why did the clock go back four seconds?

A: It was really hungry!

Q: Why did the lobster need crutches?

A: It pulled a mussel.

Q: Why did the book have to go to the hospital?

A: To have its appendix removed.

> **Jim:** I want to build a gigantic boat, but I'll need some help.
> **Bob:** Well, I just happen to Noah guy.

214

Q: When is a noodle a fake?

A: When it's an im-pasta.

Q: What has four legs but can't walk?

A: A chair.

Q: Why do silent frogs live forever?

A: Because they never croak!

Tammy: I'm embarrassed to go to the eye doctor.

Tommy: Why?

Tammy: My doctor always makes a spectacle of himself!

Q: How does a bumblebee stay out of trouble?

A: It stays on its best bee-havior.

Q: When does a hot dog get on your nerves?

A: When it's being a brat—it's the wurst.

Jimmy: Did you hear about the kid that got hit in the head with a can of pop?

Bobby: No, is he ok?

Jimmy: Yep, he's just lucky it was a soft drink.

Emma: I'm reading a book about gravity.

Leah: That's cool. Is it a good book?

Emma: It sure is! I just can't put it down.

Q: Why did the boy stop using his pencil?

A: It was pointless.

Q: Why did the ruler have a bad report card?

A: His grades just didn't measure up.

Q: Why did the wood fall asleep?

A: It was board.

Q: What do you get when you cross a train with a tissue?

A: An achoo-choo train.

Q: Why did the bee need to take allergy medicine?

A: It had lots of hives.

Q: What happens when strawberries are sad?

A: They become blueberries!

Q: What did the judge say to the skunk?

A: "Odor in the court!"

Q: Why was the potato chip mad at the pretzel?

A: Because it was insalting him.

Q: Why can you trust your secrets with a sea lion?

A: Their lips are always seal-ed!

Q: What did the lipstick say to the eye shadow?

A: "We should stop fighting and make-up!"

Q: Where do astronauts keep their sandwiches?

A: In their launch-box.

Q: Why was the man upset after he became a vegetarian?

A: He realized he'd made a missed-steak.

Sam: Did you like that story about the farm?

Sue: No, it didn't have a very good plot.

Q: Why couldn't the Cyclops family get along?

A: They could never see eye-to-eye.

Knock knock.

Who's there?

Bat.

Bat who?

I bat you want to hear some more knock-knock jokes!

Q: What did the shovel say to the sand?
A: "I really dig you!"

Q: Who helps pigs fall in love?
A: Cu-pig.

Q: How do bees get to school?
A: They take the school buzz.

Q: Why can't you tell a joke to an egg?
A: It might crack up!

Q: Why didn't the two 4's come to the dinner table?
A: Because they already 8.

Q: Why was the carpenter mad that he hit the nail with his hammer?
A: Because it was his fingernail!

Knock knock.

Who's there?

Bach.

Bach who?

I'll be Bach later when you're ready to open the door!

Knock knock.

Who's there?

Lasagna.

Lasagna who?

Are you going to lasagna couch all day, or are you going to answer the door?

Knock knock.

Who's there?

Snow.

Snow who?

What, don't you snow me?

Knock knock.

Who's there?

Bacon.

Bacon who?

Don't go bacon my heart.

Q: What kind of bugs like to sneak up on you?
A: Spy-ders.

Q: What do magicians like to eat for breakfast?
A: Trix cereal.

Knock knock.

Who's there?

Shore.

Shore who?

I shore hope you know some more knock-knock jokes!

Knock knock.

Who's there?

Minnow.

Minnow who?

Let minnow when you plan on letting me in!

Q: What kind of cars do deep-sea divers drive?
A: Scubarus.

Q: What is a whale's motto?
A: "Seas the Day."

Q: Why did the shoe fall in love with the boot?
A: Because they were sole mates.

Knock knock.

Who's there?

Roach.

Roach who?

I roach you a letter—will you write back soon?

Q: Why was the snail moving so slow?
A: It was feeling sluggish.

Q: Why did the frog get sent home from school?

A: He was a bully-frog!

Q: What happened when they invented the broom?

A: It was an idea that swept the nation!

Q: How does Moses make his tea?

A: Hebrews it.

Q: Why do cows wear cowbells?

A: Because they don't have horns.

Q: What kind of dogs are always on time?

A: Watch dogs!

Q: What is the best way to communicate with a fish?

A: Drop it a line.

Q: How does Jack Frost get around?

A: On his motor-cicle.

Q: What do you get when you cross a bear and a pig?

A: A grizzly boar!

Q: **When should you stay away from a comedian?**

A: When they want to give you the punch-line!

Q: **How did the marching band keep their teeth clean?**

A: With a tuba toothpaste.

Q: **Why wouldn't the lions play games with the zebras?**

A: There were too many cheetahs.

Q: **How do comedians like their eggs?**

A: Funny-side up.

Knock knock.

Who's there?

Moe.

Moe who?

Do you know any Moe knock-knock jokes?

Q: **Why is the ocean so much fun?**

A: You can always have a whale of a time.

Q: **When can't you believe anything a hippopotamus says?**

A: When it's a hippo-crite.

Knock knock.

Who's there?

Taco.

Taco who?

I don't want to taco 'bout it—just let me in!

Q: What did the violin say to the guitar when it was worried?

A: "Don't fret!"

Q: Why are omelets so out of shape?

A: They don't get enough eggs-ercise.

Q: Why didn't the cow have any money?

A: The farmer had milked it for all its worth!

Peter: You have got to put pickles on your sandwich!

Penny: Why, what's the big dill?

Q: What did the C note say to the D note?

A: "Stop! You're under a rest."

Q: How do you know if your printer likes music?

A: When it's always jamming.

Knock knock.

Who's there?

Bacon.

Bacon who?

Let me in—I'm bacon out here!

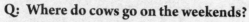

Q: **Where do cows go on the weekends?**
A: To the moo-seum.

Q: **When does a king have trouble breathing?**
A: When he doesn't have any heir.

Q: **What do you give a deer with a tummy ache?**
A: Elk-aseltzer.

Q: **Why did the bear eat a lamp?**
A: It just wanted a light snack.

Q: **Where did the beaver put its money?**
A: In the river bank.

Q: **Why did the house go to the doctor?**
A: It had a lot of window panes.

Q: Why was the bee's hair all sticky?

A: It used a honeycomb.

Q: What do you get when you try a new kind of bread for the first time?

A: Meet-loaf.

Q: Why did the police arrest the chicken?

A: They suspected fowl play.

Knock knock.

Who's there?

Isaac.

Isaac who?

Isaac of these knock-knock jokes!

Q: What is a frisbee's favorite kind of music?

A: Disk-o.

Q: Why wouldn't the worm buy anything new?

A: It was dirt cheap.

Sue: Did you hear about the towel that liked to tell jokes?

Alley: Was the towel funny?

Sue: It had a dry sense of humor.

Q: Why did the pig have to sit on the bench during football practice?

A: He pulled his ham-string.

Q: What is a good thing to eat when you're feeling stressed?

A: A marsh-mellow.

Q: What kind of shoes do bakers wear?

A: Loaf-ers.

Q: What did the orange say when it was stepped on?

A: "You hurt my peelings!"

Q: Why were all the animals laughing at the owl?

A: Because he was a hoot!

Q: What do you get when you combine a monster and a genius?

A: Frank-Einstein.

Q: Why couldn't all the king's horses and all the king's men put Humpty Dumpty together again?

A: They were eggshausted.

Q: What did the composer say after the symphony?

A: "I'll be Bach."

Q: What do frogs eat on a really hot day?

A: Hop-sicles.

Q: Why did the boy always carry his piggy bank outside?

A: In case there was change in the weather.

Q: Why was the math teacher sad?

A: He had a lot of problems to solve.

Q: How did the police know the invisible man was lying?

A: They could see right through him.

Q: Why did the cat like to go bowling?

A: It was an alley cat.

Q: Why do basketball players need so many napkins?

A: They're always dribbling!

Q: Why did the bird go to the hospital?

A: To get medical tweetment.

Q: Why did the monkey go to the golf course?

A: So it could practice its swing.

Q: Where do bees go when they get married?

A: On their honey-moon.

Q: What do you call a bear with no socks?

A: Bear-foot.

Q: When can't you trust a farmer?

A: When he spills the beans!

Q: What do you call a cowboy that falls off his horse?

A: An OW-boy!

Q: Where do ducks live in the city?

A: In their pond-ominiums.

Q: What kind of animal has the best eyesight?

A: A see lion.

Q: How did the tuba call the trumpet?

A: On his saxo-phone.

Q: What do you call a really big insect?

A: A gi-ant.

Q: How did the barber win the race?

A: He took a short-cut.

Q: Where do polar bears go to vote?

A: The North Poll.

Q: What did the baby corn say to the mommy corn?

A: "Where is Pop-corn?"

Knock knock.

Who's there?

Lava.

Lava who?

I lava you!

Q: What do bumblebees play at the park?

A: Fris-bee.

Q: Why do gorillas have big fingers?

A: Because they have big nostrils.

Q: What did the doe say to the fawn when it was naughty?

A: "The buck stops here!"

Q: Why are sheep so gullible?

A: It's easy to pull the wool over their eyes.

Q: What did the hat say to the scarf?

A: "You hang around here for a while—I'm going to go ahead."

Q: When does the alphabet only have 24 letters?

A: When U and I are not part of it!

Q: What kind of photographs do dentists take?

A: Tooth pics.

Q: When is a dinosaur boring to hang around with?

A: When it's a dino-snore.

Q: What happened to the cow when it lost its GPS?

A: It became udderly lost!

Vicki: Do you want to hear my joke about pizza?

Leah: Not really!

Vicki: Well, it was kind of cheesy anyway!

Knock knock.

Who's there?

Owl.

Owl who?

Owl wait right here until you open the door!

Q: How do clams call home?

A: They use their shell phones!

Q: What do monsters sing at the ball game?

A: The national phantom.

Q: Why can't you invite pigs to your birthday party?

A: They might go hog wild.

Q: What do frogs wear in the summer time?

A: Open-toad shoes.

Q: What kind of sea creature needs help at school?

A: A "C" horse.

Q: What do you find at the end of everything?

A: The letter "g."

Q: What's brown and sticky?

A: A stick.

Q: Why are there frogs on the baseball team?

A: To catch the fly balls!

Samantha: Who stole the poor baby octopus?

Henry: I don't know, who?

Samantha: The squidnappers!

Q: What do snowmen like best at school?

A: Snow and tell.

Q: What do you get from grumpy cows?

A: Sour milk!

Knock knock.

Who's there?

Yam.

Yam who?

I yam glad you asked—it's me!

Justin: I had a terrible dream about horses last night.

Anna: Was it a night-mare?

Q: What do music and chickens have in common?

A: Bach, Bach, Bach!

Q: Why can't you win a race with a rope?

A: It will always end with a tie.

Knock knock.

Who's there?

Butter.

Butter who?

I butter tell you a few more knock-knock jokes.

Q: Why should you always be nice to a horse?

A: Because you should love your neigh-bor as yourself.

Q: Why don't you want to fight with a snail?

A: It might try to slug you.

Knock knock.

Who's there?

Grape.

Grape who?

It would be grape if you'd tell me some more knock-knock jokes!

Q: Where does a shark go on Saturday nights?
A: To the dive-in movies.

Q: What did the girl oyster say to the boy oyster?
A: "You always clam up when I try to talk to you!"

Q: Why can't you win an argument with a pencil?
A: It's always write.

Q: What animal can jump higher than a house?
A: All of them—houses can't jump!

Q: Why couldn't the skunk go shopping?
A: It didn't have a scent in its wallet.

Q: Why did the boat go to the mall?
A: It was looking for a sail.

Q: Should we use a rowboat or a canoe to get across the lake?

A: It's either-oar.

Q: What has 50 feet and sings?

A: A choir.

Q: What do you call a cow with two legs?

A: Lean beef.

Knock knock.

Who's there?

Whale.

Whale who?

Whale you tell me another knock-knock joke?

Knock knock.

Who's there?

Gouda.

Gouda who?

Tell me another gouda knock-knock joke.

Q: Why did the people pucker up every time they drove around town?

A: Because they were driving a lemon!

Q: How can you learn more about spiders?

A: Check out their web-site.

Q: What do you call a guy stuffed in your mailbox?

A: Bill.

> **Josh:** How do you know that eating carrots is good for your eyes?
>
> **John:** Well, have you ever seen a rabbit with glasses before?

> **Margie:** Would you like to go camping this weekend?
>
> **Minnie:** No, that sounds too in-tents for me.

Q: What happens when you cross a river and a stream?

A: You get wet feet!

Q: What is smarter than a talking cat?

A: A spelling bee.

Q: Why did the bunny go to the hospital?

A: It needed a hop-eration.

Q: Why did the reporter go to the ice cream parlor?

A: He wanted to get the scoop!

Q: What is a drummer's favorite vegetable?

A: A beet.

Q: Why is it hard to carry on a conversation with rams?

A: Because they're always butting in!

Q: What kind of bear stays out in the rain?

A: A drizzly bear.

Knock knock.

Who's there?

Bean.

Bean who?

I've bean waiting for you to open the door!

Knock knock.

Who's there?

Porpoise.

Porpoise who?

Are you leaving me out here on porpoise or will you answer the door?

Knock knock.

Who's there?

Wyatt.

Wyatt who?

Wyatt is taking you so long to open the door?

Knock knock.

Who's there?

Dawn.

Dawn who?

It just Dawn-ed on me—I should tell another knock-knock joke!

Q: **Why did the duck set his alarm for so early in the morning?**

A: He liked to get up at the quack of dawn!

Q: What do you call a skeleton that isn't very smart?

A: A numbskull.

Q: What do you get when you cross a daisy and a bike?

A: Bicycle petals.

Knock knock.

Who's there?

Cook.

Cook who?

You sound a little crazy!

Knock knock.

Who's there?

Harry.

Harry who?

Harry up and answer the door, and I'll tell you another joke!

Q: Where can you learn to make ice cream treats?

A: In sundae school.

Q: Why don't math books last very long?

A: Their days are numbered.

Knock knock.

Who's there?

Nose.

Nose who?

Nobody nose a good joke when they hear one anymore!

Q: What do computer programmers eat when they're hungry?

A: Bytes of chips.

Q: Where do mermaids go for fun?

A: The dive-in movies!

Q: What kind of bird has a lot of money?

A: An ost-rich.

Q: Where is the best place to keep an angry dog?

A: In the grrrrage.

Q: What kind of coat is always wet and colorful?

A: A coat of paint!

Q: **Why did the bat join the circus?**

A: So it could be an acro-bat.

Knock knock.

Who's there?

Wheel.

Wheel who?

Wheel you let me tell you another knock-knock joke?

Knock knock.

Who's there?

Mark Twain.

Mark Twain who?

You mark my words, the twain will be here soon!

Q: **What kind of shoes do monsters wear?**

A: Combat boo-ts!

Q: **What do garbage collectors eat for lunch?**

A: Junk food!

Q: **What kind of bird always shows up at dinnertime?**

A: A swallow.

Q: What's a lion's favorite day of the week?

A: Chewsday.

Q: How do elk know it's hunting season?

A: They check their calen-deer!

Q: What did the snowman say to Jack Frost?

A: "Have an ice day!"

Q: What is a golfer's favorite drink?

A: Iced tee.

Q: What do you wear to play mini-golf?

A: A tee-shirt.

Q: How do porcupines stay warm in the winter?

A: They cover up with a quill-t!

Q: What kind of dogs chop down trees?

A: Lumber Jack Russells.

Knock knock.

Who's there?

Turnip.

Turnip who?

Turnip the heat—it's cold out here!

Q: **What kind of cars do monsters drive?**
A: Doom buggies.

Q: **What did the lamb want to be when she grew up?**
A: A baaaa-llerina.

Q: **How can you tell when a bell is old?**
A: It has ring-kles.

Q: **What did the cell phone say to the landline?**
A: "Hi, Grandma!"

Q: **What is a rat's favorite website?**
A: Mice-space.

Q: **What does a clam wear to the gym?**
A: A mussel shirt.

Q: Why did the snake cross the road?

A: To get to the other sssssss-ide!

Q: What is the cleanest state?

A: Wash-ington!

Knock knock.

Who's there?

Water.

Water who?

Water you doing later?

Q: What's black and white and goes around, around, and around?

A: A penguin stuck in a revolving door!

Q: Why do penguins carry fish in their beaks?

A: They don't have any pockets.

Q: What do you get when you put your notebook in your bed?

A: Sheets of paper!

Q: What do you get when you step on a piano?

A: Foot-notes!

Q: **How does the snowman like his root beer?**

A: In a frosted mug.

Q: **What does Jack Frost call his parents?**

A: Mom and Pop-sicle!

Q: **Why did Frosty go live in the middle of the ocean?**

A: Because snow man is an island!

Tongue Twisters

Irish wristwatch, Swiss wristwatch

Plump pink pillows

Splish splash plip plop

Coloring with crayons can cause cramps

Spunky pumpkins

Good bread, bad bread

Bouncy blue beach balls

Tickling tiny turkey toes

Crispy kitty cookies

Q: What do you get when you hang a trumpet on a Christmas tree?

A: A Christmas hornament.

Q: How do crocodiles like to cook their food?

A: In a crockpot!

Knock knock.

Who's there?

Window.

Window who?

Window we get to hear another knock-knock joke?

Wade: What do you think of my rash?

Merv: It's kind of gross.

Wade: Just wait a while—it will grow on you!

Q: Why are possums so lazy?

A: All they do is hang around.

Q: Why did the billboard go to the doctor?

A: It had a sign-us infection.

Q: What do you say to a noisy jar?

A: "Put a lid on it!"

Q: What do you get when you cross a cow and a rabbit?

A: Hare in your milk!

Q: What do get when you borrow money from a cow?

A: A buffa-loan.

Knock knock.

Who's there?

Cheryl.

Cheryl who?

Cheryl be glad to tell you another knock-knock joke!

Q: What does a carpenter eat for lunch?

A: A ham-mer and cheese sandwich.

Q: What happens when you throw your vegetables in the ocean?

A: You get sea cucumbers!

Q: Why was the cow embarrassed?

A: It had become a laughing stock.

Q: Where do musicians like to kiss?

A: Under the mistle-tone.

Q: What did the fork say to the knife?

A: "No need to be so blunt!"

Q: Why wouldn't anyone talk to the bread?

A: It was a weir-dough.

Q: Where does a horse go when it's sick?

A: To the horse-pital.

Knock knock.

Who's there?

Ache.

Ache who?

God bless you!

Q: What happened after the man accidently dropped his coffee in the volcano?

A: Java came out!

Q: What did the pen say to the pencil?

A: "Get the lead out!"

Q: What do skunks sing at Christmas time?

A: "Jingle smells, jingle smells."

Q: Why did the calendar have such a great attitude?

A: It was taking life one day at a time!

Knock knock.

Who's there?

Owl.

Owl who?

I'm owl by myself, please let me in.

Q: Why was the bird always crying?

A: Because it was a blue bird!

Q: What do bugs need to do their homework?

A: An ant-cyclopedia.

Q: What do you get when you combine an elephant and an insect?

A: An eleph-ant.

Q: What did the bread say to the baker?

A: "I need you to knead me."

Q: Why was the skeleton laughing?

A: Because he found his humerus.

Knock knock.

Who's there?

Token.

Token who?

Now that's what I'm token about!

Q: What do frogs order when they go to fast food restaurants?

A: French flies and croak-a-cola.

Anna: **Was that a skeleton at the door?**

Leah: No, it was no body.

Q: Why was the whale always bragging?

A: Because it was fishing for compliments.

Q: What do black bears wear in their hair?

A: Bearrettes.

Q: What kind of fish comes out at night?

A: A starfish.

Q: What makes bananas such great drivers?

A: They're always keeping their eyes peeled.

Q: What did the mouse say to the rat at the movies?

A: "The squeakuel is never as good as the original."

Q: Why is jelly always so much fun?

A: Because it's always jamming.

Q: Why was the sheep practicing karate?

A: Because it was a lamb chop!

Q: What kind of clothing do disobedient children wear?

A: They wear smarty-pants.

Q: Where do fish get their money?

A: From the loan shark.

Q: How do ants cook their food?

A: With a micro-wave!

Q: How do you have a party on Mars?

A: You have to planet.

Rob Elliott has been a publishing professional for more than twenty years and lives in West Michigan, where in his spare time he enjoys laughing out loud with his wife and four children.